Oh @#$% I'm Graduating!

A Student's Guide to Creating a Killer Portfolio

Oh @#$% I'm Graduating!

A Student's Guide to Creating a Killer Portfolio

Ben Hannam

Diane Gibbs
Contributing Author

Kendall Hunt
publishing company

Cover Design by Drew Ellis
Cover Photography by Randy Piland

www.kendallhunt.com
Send all inquiries to:
4050 Westmark Drive
Dubuque, IA 52004-1840

Copyright © 2018 by Kendall Hunt Publishing Company

ISBN: 978-1-5249-4397-4

Published in the United States of America

TABLE OF CONTENTS

TABLE OF CONTENTS

Preface

Oh @#$% I'm Graduating! A Student's Guide to Creating a Killer Portfolio is a book to help students create a unique and targeted visual portfolio. Most design professionals agree that the quality of a candidate's portfolio is one of the single biggest factors in determining who gets offered a job and who doesn't. In fact, the quality of a candidate's portfolio can even be more important than the grade point average, academic major or minor, an internship, or work experience. Simply put, your portfolio is where the rubber hits the road and you demonstrate that you can not only talk the talk, but that you also walk the walk. Simply put, your portfolio speaks to your credibility.

As a professor, empowering students with the tools they need to succeed as they transition from an academic to a professional environment is a passion of mine. This book was written to complement a book I previously authored titled, *A Graphic Design Student's Guide to Freelance: Practice Makes Perfect,* and you might notice that both books share a 'you can do this,' encouraging tone. This is because I've been practicing what I've been preaching for over 15 years and semester after semester I've seen my students exceed their expectations time and time again. If you arm yourself with a good plan and get pumped up for the challenge, then I feel confident that you are going to exceed your own expectations and be pleased with the portfolio you create for yourself.

While this book was written from a graphic designer's perspective, the content is appropriate for students in many disciplines including studio arts, marketing, strategic communications, public relations, and so forth. The strategies, theories, and resources discussed can be used in many disciplines and can be embraced, modified, and edited for your own needs, to help make your work stand out, and amplify your narrative. Graphic design is a profession that unabashedly borrows from many other disciplines and many of the tools that designers use can also be used by other disciplines to help focus your narrative and improve your results.

I have taught Graphic Design for over 15 years, and when I went looking for books to use as a resource for my senior-level capstone class, I purchased over ten books about portfolios and found they fell into one of two basic categories. The books fell into a 'portfolio showcase' or an 'about portfolio' categories. Neither of these two types of categories matched the discussions I was having with my students inside the classroom. I set out to author a textbook that included a much needed section on how to create a strategy for your portfolio in order to position yourself (and your work) in the best light possible.

When I was in school putting together your portfolio consisted of reprinting examples of our best work, mocking up projects with impeccable craftsmanship, and mounting everything neatly into a rather large portfolio. Unfortunately, it seems both the expectations for entry-level employees and the competition for entry-level jobs have increased over the years.

You don't have to be clairvoyant to know that the days of creating a generic portfolio are just about over. Advancements in technology, elevated competition, changes in business protocols, and employer expectations have changed over the last twenty years. It also won't surprise you to hear that the criteria for building a visual portfolio have changed as well. These days in order to compete for a job you have to package yourself in a very targeted and strategic way.

In order to create an effective and eye-catching portfolio you need to start by better understanding the needs of your audience—your potential employer. In its simplest form, putting together your portfolio is no different than any other design project you've worked on. You start by defining your problem and understanding your audience, create a series of sketches and brainstorming sessions to generate ideas, identify any constraints you have to work around, execute and test your ideas, gather feedback, and evaluate your efforts. It sounds so simple, doesn't it? Unfortunately, when it comes to branding ourselves many students and designers alike often suffer from 'paralysis by analysis.' We tend to overthink, second guess, and question our efforts and we either don't get much done or we don't feel confident about our decisions. When this happens it's important to realize that while a portfolio represents your narrative, efforts, and accomplishments— *you aren't building your portfolio for you*. It's important to understand that you're building your portfolio for a hiring manager, creative director, graduate school committee, and so forth. Your goal isn't to capture *all* the complex and wonderful things about yourself in visual form as much as it is to create a narrative that connects your skills and passions to the needs of your audience.

When I remember my job isn't to communicate everything about myself I feel like a little bit of the load is lifted and I hope you feel that way too. When I can put my finger on the narrative I need to create for a particular employer I think to myself, "Hey, I can do this!" When I get far enough along that my visual voice begins to emerge and I start feeling confident about my research, I begin to feel excited about talking with the art director. Feeling prepared and confident walking into an interview is a great feeling, and that in a nutshell is what this book is all about—getting you to that place where you're happy with your work and ready to share your portfolio.

When you can put a strategy together that is unique to you, create work that appeals to your audience, curate and brand your portfolio in an intelligent and creative way, and land the job—you know you've created a killer portfolio. That, in a nutshell, is my goal for you. To help empower and equip you with the tools, wisdom, and strategies you need to succeed.

If my students can graduate from a small graphic design program and go on to get jobs at well-known companies, get accepted into great graduate schools, and open up their own agencies, then you can do it too. While every step along the way might not feel terribly comfortable, you'll look back at where you are right now in a few weeks and you'll be amazed at how far you've come. I won't lie and tell you that it'll be easy, but you'll be glad that you rolled up your sleeves and dug deep.

Many of my students start off strong, begin to fade around midterms, and have to dig deep to finish by the end of the semester. The best strategy I've found is to chip away at the problem consistently over time. Just like runners who run a 10k race, you've got to pace yourself and save a little energy for the end of the race. While you might feel like crushing as much work as possible right out of the gate, sometimes it takes a little time for concepts and ideas to take hold. Don't rush the process, and most importantly—don't skip out on writing the research paper. While it might not feel like you're getting much accomplished on your portfolio when you're writing your paper, you're basically planning your attack and helping focus your efforts.

You can do this and you're going to be great at it. Buckle up because the next few weeks are going to go by quickly. If you're a person who feels anxious easily, then you'll need to remind yourself to take one step at a time. We're going to demystify the portfolio building process and break it up into manageable steps. By the time you reach midterms your portfolio will have begun to take shape and you'll be able to tell how much work you have left to do. You've totally got this!

Acknowledgments

I would like to express my sincere thanks and gratitude to the many individuals who have made this book possible. Many of my views about graphic design and life have been shaped by friends, family, colleagues, and students, and I am deeply grateful for your hard work, kind words, constructive criticism, and encouragement.

I would like to thank my family—Julie, Ruby, and Beckett for their love, patience, and support. My family has encouraged and supported me through both my successes and failures and given me the courage to "Go big, fail big." Thank you so much for all of your support over the years.

It's also been my pleasure to work with such great colleagues and administration in the School of Communication at Elon University. I'd especially like to thank Paul Parsons, Don Grady, Jessica Gisclair, Harlen Makemson, Amanda Sturgill, and Phillip Motley among many others for their guidance and support. I'd also like to thank my students who have generously allowed me to publish their work in this book and have helped shape the narrative of this textbook in so many ways.

I'd like to thank my contributing author, Diane Gibbs for all of her hard work and patience. Diane you are an amazing designer, educator, and leader—I feel very privileged to call you my friend. Thank you for introducing me to so many of your talented and extremely creative friends.

Finally, I'd also like to thank Brittanie Tucker, Connor Schreck, Torrie Johnson, and all the wonderful staff at Kendall Hunt. Thank you for answering my many questions and working with me to complete this book. I hope you have enjoyed this experience as much as I have. You have been wonderful to work with and I hope to work with you again in the future. Thank you for all your hard work and encouragement.

1. Your Portfolio

When I was eight years old my father took me to see *Star Wars Episode IV: A New Hope*, and over the years we went to see several of the Star Wars films together. I looked forward to watching these movies with my dad, and we always enjoyed it when new characters were introduced into the series.

After a long eight year wait the trailer for *Episode VII: The Force Awakens* came out. The antagonist, Darth Vader, had died and Star Wars fans were introduced to a new villain for the very first time. Fans nearly lost their minds with anticipation as the movie trailer revealed Kylo Ren, wielding a lightsaber, the likes of which fans had never seen before.

Kylo Ren's lightsaber had a crossguard on it and quite literally made Star Wars fans both young and old do a double take. Fans hit the Internet forums with speculation, questions, and theories about the new lightsaber. In fact, the fans exerted so much pressure for information that J.J. Abrams was forced to comment on the lightsaber design before the movie had even been released.

Abrams said, "It was a number of conversations that led to the design. It was a sketch that became a whole thing and, you know, this was not done without a lot of conversation, and it's fun to see people have the conversation that we had."

The hook had been set, and Star Wars fans knew they were in for a real treat. Anticipation grew as the date of the opening approached.

> *"I love it when design can do that—inform who the character is."*
> —*Doug Chiang*

In an interview with Yahoo Movies, Doug Chiang a concept artist who had worked on the new lightsaber commented:

> Early on, J.J. had always described Kylo as this next-generation villain who's going to be as bad as Vader, and as powerful. And he said he's kind of like a knight, a dark knight. So it works well, that the blade has a crossguard. You bring in those little elements that start to reflect the character. I love it when designs can do that, inform who the character is. And at the same time, I remember when I first saw the crossguard on the lightsaber, it put a smile on my face. It was so unexpected but felt right.

According to Cinemablend, an online blog, "The crossguard design was something that had never been seen on screen before, and many fans viewed the idea as impractical. But the design was necessary as a way to tell you more about the character." Doug Chiang had managed to set the stage for the next series of Star Wars movies and bolster the interest of fans with a single prop.

THE PORTFOLIO METAPHOR

If you are a fan of the Star Wars films, then you might remember that each Jedi knight designs his or her lightsaber. The design of the lightsaber typically reveals clues about their character (and sometimes their flaws) and similarly when you build your portfolio it will reflect and reveal your visual voice, personality, and decision-making abilities. Just like a unique lightsaber set the stage for the tone of a movie, your visual portfolio can help you make a strong first impression. A good portfolio shows a range of work, helps you establish your narrative, demonstrates the degree of your experience and creativity, and assists in establishing your credibility.

Look at Ryan Donnell's portfolio on the opposite page and consider what his portfolio might communicate to a hiring manager or client. Without seeing the work inside the portfolio, Ryan has anchored the viewer with the impression that he is a professional and skilled artisan. A portfolio like this suggests that he pays attention to details and isn't afraid of breaking away from conventions. Similar to how Kylo Ren's lightsaber alluded to his fractured and unstable personality, Ryan's portfolio suggests that he is the type of photographer whose work is imbued with finesse and excellent craftsmanship.

His portfolio implies that he is a creative individual and that his work is likely to be free from technical errors. Ryan comments, "I was looking for a unique carrying case for my portfolio book, something that would protect the book, be fairly easy to carry and also reasonably easy to ship. I stumbled upon some cool carrying cases that were built in Oregon by a very talented woodworker." Ryan's unique portfolio does an excellent job of creating a sense of anticipation (just like the lightsaber) before we even see the work and helps sets the bar high for how it will be perceived.

Your portfolio can speak volumes about your capabilities as an artist, designer, and so forth. Your portfolio is there to help you make an impression about your sense of style, abilities, control over the design principles, typography, and other visual elements. Your portfolio is often where you establish your personal brand and professional identity. Making good choices early on is a critical step to creating a cohesive package.

WHERE TO BEGIN

Creating a killer portfolio starts with the idea that "Your portfolio isn't for you." Let me explain. You are creating a portfolio that is filled with strategically chosen pieces so that it will appeal to a very specific audience. It is exceedingly likely that *you* are not the audience for your portfolio and while your portfolio should represent *your* capabilities and skills, your portfolio ultimately needs to appeal to someone else.

Your very first act of creating a stunning portfolio is identifying who your audience is and what their needs are. This is a crucial first step that requires you to research your audience, talk to others, and perhaps most importantly develop a strategy you can use to focus your portfolio (and your work) in order to meet their needs.

To be successful, you will need to be thorough in your research and do some soul searching. If this seems a bit abrupt, then let me be the first to welcome you to the end of your academic career and the beginning of your professional career. This can be a scary time and leaving the safety of school can be a bittersweet experience. Over the next few chapters, we are going to demystify the portfolio building process, break it down into manageable parts, and hopefully make the entire process less stressful for you.

YOUR PORTFOLIO ISN'T FOR YOU

The odds of hitting your target go up dramatically
when you identify what you're aiming at.

2. Analyzing Your Audience

By this point in your academic career, you know how important it is to identify your audience whether you are writing a research paper, designing an advertisement, or developing a marketing campaign. It shouldn't come as a surprise that the first step in creating an impressive portfolio is to identify who you are making the portfolio for and to tailor your work to meet this audience's needs. Your goal is to help the hiring manager by making it as easy as possible for them to say, "We'd like to offer you a job." A great way to do this is to research and learn about the qualities a company is looking for and then highlight some of these same qualities in your body of work and portfolio.

> *"Without getting to know your audience and being able to clearly articulate your goals after graduation you'll be lost."*

Once you've identified your audience, you should write a paper (discussed in greater detail later) on your audience's needs and your post graduation goals. I can hear you saying, "There's no way I'm going to write a paper!" but I promise you that this time will be well spent. Without getting to know your audience and being able to clearly articulate your goals after graduation, you'll be lost. Without completing this first step your design decisions will be reduced to personal taste, the critiques you receive will be based on personal preferences, and the underlying narrative of your portfolio may lack relevance.

To be clear, I'm asking you to write about what fulfillment looks like to you and what breaking into your chosen profession looks like. These revelations are going to serve as the problems you're attempting to solve with your portfolio.

Google isn't going to solve this problem for you.

> *"The <u>more specific</u> you can be about your <u>professional goals</u>, the better. Self-awareness and ample research is key."*

DO I REALLY NEED TO WRITE A PAPER?

Over the next few months, you are going to have to make a lot of decisions and you are going to refer to this paper time and time again in order to help you make good design decisions. Not only will writing a paper help you to be better informed, but it will help you make better choices more quickly and confidently later.

There are only a few types of documents (see the list below) that you have at your disposal to help you make a positive impression with a potential employer, and all of these items need to work together to communicate why you are the best candidate for a particular position. To create a cohesive package, it's essential that you have some over-arching plan to guide you and keep you on track. So yes, in my professional opinion you need to write a paper. Better yet, you need to write a really good paper.

Documents to Help Establish Your Credentials

- Your portfolio
- Your résumé
- Your website
- Your branding system
- A cover letter
- A leave-behind item

IDENTIFYING YOUR GOALS

Your first objective in writing this paper is one that is <u>based on self-awareness</u> and <u>determining what fulfillment looks like to you</u>. You'll need to identify what type of job will be both obtainable and enjoyable to do after you graduate. Being specific about what this job looks like is critical because saying something like, "I want to go into graphic design" is far too broad. Instead, try to be more precise and say something like, "I want to work at a small <u>design agency</u> in either Richmond, Virginia or Raleigh, North Carolina. I'm interested in working with a variety of clients in a supportive, team-based environment where I can be involved with many parts of a project. It's important that I have the opportunity to get to know my clients and establish a rapport with them."

A statement like this is extremely <u>helpful for your professor and classmates to consider when critiquing the work in your portfolio</u>. Also, this revelation allows you to begin to compile a list of agencies that meet your ideal criteria, so you can begin focusing your efforts on creating a body of work that will help position yourself as a good candidate for these types of agencies.

[margin handwritten note: CONSIDERING WHAT YOU CURRENTLY DO & WHAT YOUR FUTURE GOALS ARE.]

> *"You might not be familiar with many of the job titles and their inherent duties at this point, so part of your research should be devoted to understanding the professional environment better."*

When writing about what fulfillment looks like to you, be careful about making statements like, "I want to be an art director at an award-winning agency in New York city" because the likelihood of landing this type of position right out of school is mathematically slim. Typically, these types of positions require you to cut your teeth and gain industry experience before jumping into a leadership role, so set realistic expectations for yourself.

If you truly want to be an art director in New York, you might want to scale down your expectations a bit and think about your first job out of college as your first move, in a series of strategic moves, to help you land your dream job. Not only will the chances of achieving your goal increase, but your time and resources will be better utilized as well.

TALKING WITH PROFESSIONALS

You might not be familiar with many of the job titles and duties at this point, so part of your research should be devoted to understanding the professional environment a bit better. If you aren't sure what the difference between a 'design strategist' and a 'graphic designer' is, then this paper presents you with an opportunity to dig deeper into some of the nuances within your profession. Not only that, but a big component of this writing assignment is to talk with at least two professionals who hold the type of position you are interested in applying for once you graduate.

Talking with professionals may be one of the most uncomfortable steps you are asked to take, but you can learn tons of useful information to help you make more informed choices. Stop for a moment and think about how many students don't take this step and how advantageous it could be for one brave soul—like yourself—to gain a strategic advantage by conducting some research.

The conversations you have with these professionals are likely to make an indelible mark on you, helping you determine how to brand yourself and decide what work you should include in your portfolio. The point is, you have very little to lose and a whole lot to gain by talking with professionals. Reaching out to talk with professionals doesn't have to be a big deal, but it's a step most students are unwilling to make. Once you've done it, you'll probably feel a little silly for worrying about it so much.

Give yourself a deadline to reach out to at least two professionals who hold the type of position you are most interested in. Having action items on the calendar can help motivate you into action—two weeks is plenty of time to make arrangements to talk to two professionals.

I've found that breaking down the process of identifying and contacting a professional into a few simple steps can help alleviate some of the initial fears you might be feeling. Here are a few easy steps you can take.

STEP 1: LEVERAGING YOUR RESOURCES

You might not realize it, but there are a number of resources at your disposal you can use to find professionals to talk with. The easiest and safest place to begin is by talking to your professors. As a full-time faculty member I'm often surprised at how many hours I spend sitting in my office alone during open office hours while students are elsewhere struggling. I love getting to know my students and helping them achieve their goals, but as a student it's your job to initiate these conversations, so don't be shy and ask your professor for help if you need it. Even if you don't know a professor very well, the majority of faculty members are usually very willing to talk to students and help you make connections to others in your profession.

Similarly, your school's internship office and alumni network is a great way to identify some student-friendly professionals. Your school's internship office probably has a list of individuals who have been flagged as being particularly receptive to student inquiries and alumni are usually very patient and kind. Since you are paying tuition, it makes a great deal of sense to try to leverage the resources you are paying for first.

> *"...simply making yourself available is an easy way to get your foot in the door and establish connections."*

Once you've exhausted the options available to you through your school, search for local and regional professional organizations in your respective discipline. These organizations are generally student friendly and can often help you make industry connections. Many organizations hold mixers and events where you can meet and talk with professionals in a casual setting. These type of events are usually a lot of fun to participate in and can help you identify allies quickly.

If you find a professional organization that interests you, follow the organizations through various social media channels and sign up for any newsletters or e-mail blasts to stay up-to-date on upcoming events. Many organizations need help setting up and breaking down events so if you aren't afraid to offer assistance, you'll find them appreciative to offers of help. You never know who you'll end up working with in a situation like this, but simply making yourself available is an easy way to get your foot in the door and establish connections.

If you haven't had any luck by this point, or you are unsatisfied with your results, you can contact business professionals directly. This type of unsolicited calling, or cold-calling, is largely hit or miss. If you need to cold call someone plan ahead and try to call on a day and time that is likely to be the most convenient for the person you are trying to reach. Ask if they have 15 or 20 minutes to talk with you, or if they would prefer if you called back at a more convenient time. It's generally considered good form to stick to the amount of time you've requested and to also provide the individual with an opportunity to wrap up the conversation after the agreed upon amount of time has passed.

If you decide to cold call someone at an agency directly, call the agency's main number and talk to the secretary first. You might say something like, "Hello, my name is (your name) and I am a student at (your school). I was wondering if I could talk to someone working in (job title) for a few minutes? I'm getting ready to graduate (your school) and I'm putting my portfolio together and I have a few quick questions. Is there any way you can direct me to someone who would be willing to talk with me for a few minutes?"

Even if the answer you receive is, 'No' it's important to be courteous and never be rude to an employee—especially the administrative assistant. One of my students gave the secretary at a local design agency a little attitude and the secretary reported the event to the owner of the agency. The owner called the student back and said that he would never hire someone who treated his employees this way.

Never talk rudely to an employee—especially the secretary.

Even though making a request like this can feel awkward, you might be surprised at how accommodating people can be. These professionals were once in your shoes and they know how difficult it can be to break into a profession. If you are pleasant and respectful, you are likely to receive at least a few positive responses to your requests. While you shouldn't expect everyone to roll out the red carpet for you, it's likely that someone will talk with you. Just remember that many professionals are busy, overcommitted, and need to focus on running their business, so don't take an 'I'm sorry' response personally. If a professional is unable to talk with you, tell them *"I appreciate your time and I totally understand that you're busy. Do you happen to know of anyone else that might be able to talk with me?"* and get a referral instead!

STEP 2: MAKING CONTACT

If I can offer one piece of advice to you it's this: **CALL** your professionals and talk with them on the phone—do not email them! Sending an email, Snap Chat, LinkedIn, Facebook, text message, or carrier pigeon is too impersonal and you are going to have far better results talking to them over the phone.

A phone conversation is not only quicker than typing out a thoughtful response to your questions, but it is also harder to ignore. Every semester I have students who 'feel weird' about calling a professional on the phone and want to email them instead. These are generally the same students who ask for an extension because their contact hasn't responded to their email yet.

When I asked my students why they feel weird about calling on the phone they usually indicate they are afraid that they'll say something stupid or that they won't make a good impression. Some students have even said that they don't want to 'let the cat out of the bag' because they would like to apply for a position at this agency once their portfolio materials are complete. Unfortunately, none of these are great reasons why students shouldn't talk to professionals on the phone.

Responses like this are exactly why you need to get out of your own head and ground your ideas in reality! Think about this from an employer's perspective instead of a student-centered perspective. A student calls asking for 15 minutes of your time in order to understand how to make themselves a better candidate for a position. That's not an entirely bad thing, right? The student is polite, appreciative of your time, and introduces himself and asks you to share your thoughts on breaking into a profession that they too are passionate about. This shows that the student values your opinions and believes you might be able to offer some sage advice. The student's questions are focused and he is conscious of your time. At the 15-minute mark he comments that he realizes that he's

11.
THOU SHALT NOT WIMP OUT & EMAIL.

> *"Your strategy here is two-fold: first you want to make sure that you are still interested in this type of position, and second, gather information that you can use to give you an advantage later."*

reached the end of the agreed upon time. This shows that he has good time management, attention to detail, and appreciates the time you've given him. What's not to love? While you might be feeling very self-conscious about the conversation, it's entirely possible that the employer might be impressed by your planning, questions, and thoroughness.

Email, and other forms of communication, are much harder mediums to convey subtle, emphasized, or emotional messages. While it might seem scarier to talk to someone on the phone initially you'll end up getting more detailed information, more quickly, than any way aside from a face-to-face conversation. Even if you stumble or slip up during a phone call, you can usually take a deep breath and recover without much effort. While you want to appear organized, this isn't a job interview—it's just a conversation.

STEP 3: PRE-WRITING YOUR QUESTIONS

Many students find it helpful to write out some of their questions before they pick up the phone and call. Preparing questions can make you look focused and intelligent, but resist the urge to simply read off your list of questions one after the other. Students in my classes have gotten the best results when they have their questions in front of them, but allow the conversation to flow naturally. When the opportunity presents itself they interject one of their questions when it makes the most sense.

You will probably find that 15 minutes goes by extremely quickly, and writing out your questions may help you keep the conversation on track because you'll be able to see what questions have gone unanswered. Let's be honest, the professional isn't going to provide you with a set of instructions to follow in order to get a job, but they might be able to give you some insights and boots-on-the-ground wisdom you can benefit from.

Your goal is to have a conversation and ask about their job. Try not to ask questions you already know the answers to. For example, "What have you been working on recently?" or "What is the hiring process like?" are great questions to ask. Your strategy here is two-fold: first you want to make sure you are still interested in this type of position, and second, gather information that you can use to give you a small advantage later. This is a great opportunity to ask the questions that matter to you, so make sure your questions are well considered.

Last year one of my students contacted our school's internship office, and they put him in touch with an alumna who works for a well-respected advertising agency. The student talked with the alumna on the phone and learned a valuable piece of information; approximately 70% of the agency's workforce was hired through LinkedIn. What an advantage this information gave my student right out of the gate.

This type of beneficial information was totally worth the effort and my student responded by spending extra time to update and beef up his LinkedIn profile—something he wouldn't have immediately thought to do. In addition, the alumna offered to meet and critique his portfolio at the end of the semester. This invitation gave him additional incentive to create a great portfolio since he had a way to his foot in the door.

These are exactly the types of angles you're looking for when you reach out to professionals. Yes, it can 'feel weird' to talk with strangers, but the insights and opportunities that come from doing so can be really profitable.

Once you're finished talking to the professionals, make sure to sincerely thank them for their time. It's important to realize that if the agency they work for charges their clients $200/hour and the professional just talked with you for 15 minutes, then the agency just gave you a $50 gift by allowing you to talk to their employee. In the business world a little appreciation goes a long way, so don't forget to let both the agency and the professional know how much you appreciate their time and send them a handwritten thank you card. They made time for you so return the favor and let them know you appreciate it.

"Don't look now, but you're beginning to develop a strategy to capitalize on in your portfolio."

STEP 4: STOP, TAKE NOTES, REFLECT, AND SHARE

Did your conversations with professionals reveal any insights? Did it reveal any weaknesses or obstacles that you might need to try to overcome? Have your conversations pumped you up or left you feeling more confused? While everything is fresh in your mind, write down notes from your conversations and create a list of action items, priorities, and key takeaways.

Do you feel like you received any bad advice? Was there anything they said you didn't understand? This is a great time to share with your classmates how your conversations went, and talk about some of the highlights and lowlights of your conversations. Listen while others describe their experience and what insights they've taken away from this experience. You might hear some new information, so be prepared to learn from your classmates' experiences and ask about any questions you might have.

As your class shares the results of their conversations take note on any relevant advice and any comments or advice that seems to be repeated. Don't look now, but you're beginning to develop a strategy to capitalize on in your portfolio. Granted it's not fully developed yet, but the takeaways from your interviews and your answers to the question 'what does fulfillment look like to you' should begin to align.

The needs of your audience may also be beginning to take shape and before long you'll use this information to make better decisions about the tone, content, and form your portfolio should take. These important portfolio-making decisions are no longer strictly rooted in personal preference, but in a greater understanding of your audience. You've taken a big first step at getting out of your own head and becoming empathetic to your audience's needs.

SECOND GUESSING YOURSELF

Often it's the little things that can quickly derail the best laid plans, so this paper represents an opportunity to reflect on your past, present, and future goals and weave all of the pieces together. It's not an easy process, but it's a necessary one because employers want to see that you aren't just talking the talk. They want to see what you are passionate about and how these passions have influenced your journey. It's important to be honest with yourself—even if you are beginning to have second thoughts about the job you

YOUR PORTFOLIO IS FOR THEM

Don't make your professor act like a drill instructor.
Get your paper squared away!

thought you wanted initially. Learning what you don't want to do can be as helpful as discovering what you are passionate about.

I taught a student who was really excited about going to graduate school to pursue her MFA. She contacted the schools she was interested in attending and interviewed a couple of graduate students who were attending the school. After talking with a few students she quickly realized that the reality of graduate school didn't match the expectations of what graduate school would be like. My student came back and told me that she had changed her mind about graduate school and she was worried that I would be upset with her. Instead of being upset with her, I was happy for her because she had just saved herself thousands of dollars, hundreds of hours, and plenty of mixed emotions.

Don't get me wrong, I'm a big fan of higher education, but you have to be ready, driven, and motivated to take this step. If you realize early on that a certain direction isn't right for you, then you have an opportunity to readjust your course. I'm as equally thrilled for this self-realization as I am upon hearing from a student who is pumped up about working in their discipline because their choices have suddenly been confirmed.

No matter if you are feeling self-assured or left feeling like you need to readjust your strategy, you will have a better sense of what might (and might not) make you feel fulfilled professionally. This is an important realization, because if you had jumped into making a portfolio without first identifying your goal you may have wasted a lot of time and money and ended up dissatisfied with your results in the end.

COMMITTING TO YOUR FUTURE

By now you should have an ample amount of information to clearly articulate your post-graduation goals. You probably have a collection of tidbits and strategies that you didn't think of before, and lots of helpful ideas and suggestions from talking with the professionals, your professor, and your classmates. It's time to put all of these items together in a coherent, well-articulated paper.

Begin by identifying what your plans are after graduation. Be specific and describe what is it about *this* job that appeals to you. You're building a portfolio to help you land *this* job, not building a portfolio to help get you the job you'd love to have years from now. Next, identify specific agencies and environments that are likely to be a good fit for you. Do they allow you to work in a collaborative environment? Is there something in particular about the company culture that appeals to you? Does the type of work they do excite you? What strategies should you consider with regard to the type of work you put in your portfolio? Is there a particular medium or format you should consider when constructing your portfolio?

As you write your paper, avoid creating a transcript of your conversation, but summarize key points and helpful insights in your own words. How long has the person you interviewed been in that position? What did they like most about their job? Did they give you any odd or insightful advice? How can you integrate some of the advice they gave you into your portfolio? What did they do to land their job? Summarize your takeaways from your conversations and then transition to questions that you had that weren't answered or came about as a result of having these conversations. If you were to follow up with this individual again, what questions would you ask them?

Finally, conclude your paper with your action items that you need to adopt. Identify the angles you will take to create a strong impression. These are the 'nuggets of wisdom' you worked so hard to identify. Try to deconstruct their significance and articulate why they might be important to consider implementing.

Writing a paper may seem a bit impractical at first, but pretty soon you're going to be overwhelmed with decisions and you will be able to refer back to this paper where you established your goals in order to remind yourself what messages you need to convey in your portfolio. While your plans can still change and be adjusted if necessary, taking the time to articulate your goals will help you immensely in the coming weeks. Every element in your portfolio from here on should help you advance your purpose of connecting with your audience and meeting their needs in a meaningful, creative, and articulate way. If an element in your portfolio doesn't help achieve this goal, it needs to be removed.

PUTTING YOURSELF IN THEIR SHOES

Pretend for a minute that you are a hiring manager looking for new talent. You post an advertisement for a position and you suddenly have numerous applications to review. How do you hire the right person for the job? The first thing you'll do is probably look for a way to narrow the pool of candidates quickly until you reach a more manageable number and then begin to review their material.

You'll look through cover letters, resumes, and portfolios in search of candidates that have the skill set you're looking for. You're not necessarily looking for perfection, but someone who has potential to contribute to the company's success. Each of the documents you review helps paint a picture of the candidate. Small inconsistencies make you wonder about one of the candidate's attention to detail, while another's cover letter looks generic and doesn't actually say much. As you look through the documents you discover one candidate's materials not only look great, but give you the impression that he might be a real contender for the position. You dig deeper into his materials as you begin to tick off your mental checkboxes, could your search finally be over?

If you've done your job well and made it easy for the hiring manager to say, "We'd like to offer you a position" then you could be well on your way to launching your professional career. The decisions you make over the next few weeks are decisions that are likely to affect you for a long time. There's a lot on the line and it's important for you to get passionate, focused, and dig deep. You can do this.

CHAPTER REFLECTION

How on earth can you make yourself a good candidate without understanding your audience first? The definition of a 'killer portfolio' is a portfolio that gets you hired and helps you earn your paycheck. A killer portfolio isn't about how slick your work looks or if your portfolio is made out of polished stainless steel. A killer portfolio takes aim and hits its intended target with the right message. The first step in creating your own portfolio is to get to know your audience in order to make saying, *"We'd like to offer you a position"* as easy as possible.

Creating a portfolio is a big project and one that can seem intimidating at first. Over the next few chapters we'll break this task down into manageable and digestible parts, but keep in mind that you need to constantly refer back to the paper that you've written in order to make sure the message you are visually communicating is on target. You are off to a great start, but keep your momentum going because you still have a long way to go before you can sit back and relax. Pace yourself so working on your portfolio over the next few weeks won't wear you out.

ACTIONABLE ITEMS
- ☐ Articulate what professional fulfillment looks like to you after you graduate.
- ☐ Identify the type of job, agency, and environment that appeals to you.
- ☐ Write down a list of questions you'd like to ask professionals.
- ☐ Identify and talk to at least two professionals who hold the type of position that you are likely to find fulfilling.
- ☐ Write a paper to serve as an overarching document for your portfolio. You will refer back to this document as you create work for and construct your portfolio.

Manage your time and prioritize tasks with a strategic plan.

3. Strategic Planning

Your portfolio is an evaluation tool, meaning its purpose is to provide employers an idea about your skill sets and abilities. In the previous chapter you were asked to identify your audience and in this chapter, you're going to develop a strategic plan to determine what to communicate to this audience. It's highly likely that you have a variety of talents and abilities, but identifying which of these your audience is most interested in will help you make the strongest impression.

A good portfolio will communicate something about the person who created it. For instance, a portfolio might reveal a bit about a person's interests, sense of humor, or passions. For example, a portfolio that has lots of work for nonprofit clients may communicate that this person is 'socially conscious.' If that person prints on recycled paper with soy-based inks, then it may communicate that he or she is 'environmentally friendly.' Assuming the work in the portfolio is at an acceptable level, a hiring manager is left to decide if 'socially conscious' and 'environmentally friendly' are good qualities for a candidate to possess. If the answer is 'no' then the hiring manager might continue looking through portfolios until he or she finds more of the qualities they are looking for.

Matching your strengths with a company's needs is where your research and interviews can begin to pay off. We're going to assume for now that the work in your portfolio is fantastic, but take a moment and consider what are some of the most important secondary messages that you need to communicate about yourself to an employer? Is it the fact that some of your design solutions have been professionally printed? *Probably not*. Is it your unbridled enthusiasm and work ethic? *You are getting warmer*. It may be one of the qualities, attitudes, or insights the professionals you interviewed alluded to when you talked with them. This quality might be the thing that is challenging for a company to teach, but something they look for in a good candidate.

> *"You need to make strategic decisions about your portfolio rather than adopting a throw-your-work-at-the-wall-and-see-what-sticks type of philosophy."*

Go back through your notes and reread your paper again and try to put your finger on what this quality, attribute, or insight might be. Is it curiosity? Your perseverance? Your good judgment? Or maybe something else. Whatever it is, including elements in your portfolio that speak to this quality may help make a hiring manager's decision to say "We'd like to offer you a position" easier.

In many cases, hiring managers will meet your portfolio before they meet you. Your portfolio can help build interest and anticipation, or have the opposite effect and curtail it. For this reason, it's imperative that you understand and control what you are communicating about yourself (at both the primary and secondary level) because first impressions are paramount and establish a tone. Every element in your portfolio from your choice of typefaces to your ability to craft an experience communicates, so put your efforts into the right places by being strategic with your decisions.

If it's important for your portfolio to focus on a particular area of specialization, then a portfolio that demonstrates control over a variety of areas may be less efficient. If a job requires you to show evidence of your problem-solving abilities and ability to adapt to a variety of visual styles and mediums, then a portfolio that is highly specialized may be ineffective. The point is, you need to make strategic decisions about your portfolio rather than adopting a throw-your-work-at-the-wall-and-see-what-sticks type of philosophy.

A PORTFOLIO COMMUNICATES

A portfolio is a compilation of material that exemplifies your beliefs, skills, qualifications, education, training, and experience. It provides insight into your personality and understanding into how you research, analyze, and break down a problem, iterate potential solutions, synthesize ideas, problem-solve, and develop a solution. It can also demonstrate a range of visual styles, project types, and mediums, as well as validate one's proficiency at using the design principles, gestalt theory, grid and identity systems, typography, copywriting, and elements to solve problems.

A portfolio typically contains between 8 to 20 portfolio pieces, but this number is largely determined by 1) the needs of the audience and 2) the strength and depth of the candidate's work. The consensus among most professionals is that it's a better strategy to

What is this an image of?

If someone asked you to describe the image above, how would you describe it? Some people might say it's a cross, while others say it's an arrow. Technically speaking the image above is seven white dots, but why do we see more than this? How come we see this arrangement as a cross or perhaps something else?

You may have heard the phrase, "The whole is greater than the sum of its parts," and this is a good example of this concept in action. The image above is seven white dots, but your brain assigned these dots meaning. After all, the dots appear to be aligned in a particular way for a reason, right? Your brain is trying to sort out this configuration, so it assigns meaning to the composition based on a variety of psychological factors. Your brain's job is to decode the data your five senses send to it in order to make sense of the data, communicate, and navigate your environment.

Imagine for a moment if each of the dots above were a piece in your portfolio. Each piece could be looked at individually, but you could also argue that the collection of portfolio pieces could be critiqued as a whole too. When you begin choosing the work in your portfolio you'll not only need to consider the strength of each piece individually, but you'll have to think about how all your pieces work together.

This is where the strategic planning comes into play because a killer portfolio is one where the micro- and macro-interpretations of your work complement each other and create a cohesive and relevant impression of you. Your portfolio has the potential to communicate on a variety of levels, so a good strategic plan helps you focus your efforts and is likely to save you time, money, and energy down the road. Make sure your micro- and macro-interpretations complement each other.

"The consensus among most professionals is that it's a better strategy to put fewer strong pieces of work in your portfolio than it is to include weaker projects. Bigger isn't necessarily better."

put fewer solid pieces of work in your portfolio than it is to aim for a certain total number of pieces by including weaker projects. Bigger isn't necessarily better. Generally speaking, weaker projects do more harm than good, even if it means having less work in your portfolio—editing and curating your work is an important consideration.

The visuals in your portfolio need to tell your story and should communicate the type of work you are passionate about. Moreover, you should only include the work you are proud of and prepared to discuss in greater detail.

I recently participated in the Raleigh, North Carolina Chapter of The Professional Association for Design (AIGA) portfolio review, where I critiqued students' portfolios. One student, in particular, had an impressive portfolio and I was blown away by the quality of his work. When he began talking about one of the pieces in his portfolio, his body language changed notably. I told him I noticed the change and I asked him about it. He responded, "My professor likes this piece, but it's not a project that I'm particularly confident in." We talked about the project a bit more and decided if he wasn't feeling confident about the piece, he needed to replace it with another. You didn't have to be a poker player to be able to read his body language and pick up that he wasn't proud of his solution. If you find yourself feeling particularly self-conscious about a piece in your portfolio, replace the piece with a solution you are more confident in.

HELPFUL PORTFOLIO CONSIDERATIONS

- Your strongest piece should be the first piece in your portfolio. You need to capture audience's attention as quickly as possible. The rest of your work should be ordered to complement your narrative. If possible, the last piece in your portfolio should be the second strongest piece in your portfolio.
- Pay attention to hierarchy when presenting your work and use white space strategically when designing your portfolio page. White space can be used to help guide the viewer's eyes through the page in a particular order and provide areas of visual rest.
- Create (and thoughtfully use) a system for every page in your portfolio. Each piece of work in your portfolio should look unique but should give the impression that piece is part of a system.

- Give your typography careful consideration. Often typographic decisions are the difference between good design and great design. Make sure that your typographic choices communicate your sensitivity to, and control over typography.
- It's okay to put 'real work' and 'fictitious client' work in your portfolio, but ultimately the work needs to be of a high caliber. Work you created for real clients won't earn earn extra points just because it was for a real client—the work still has to look great. Similarly, work for fictitious clients is entirely appropriate, but potential employers may want to see how you deal with client constraints, so make sure some of your solutions are grounded in reality.

COMMON PITFALLS TO AVOID
- Your portfolio shouldn't be a retrospective or an attempt to show representative examples of your life's work. Your current and most applicable work is always the preferred option.
- Don't make spelling and grammar mistakes. Make sure to proofread carefully and spellcheck everything!
- Avoid lengthy descriptions of your work. Keep your writing short and to the point.
- Avoid using pixilated images, images with watermarks, and stretched or distorted images. Purchase your images, take the photos yourself, or get permission to use photographs that you did not capture yourself.
- Don't use too many typefaces. Consider choosing a font that has a large type family and offers multiple weights and styles. For example, Helvetica Neue is available in Regular, Italic, Bold, Bold Italic, Light, Light Italic, UltraLight, UltraLight Italic, Condensed Bold, and Condensed Black. By choosing a typeface that has a variety of type families you give yourself plenty of typographic options but your typography remains visually coherent and consistent.
- Avoid putting your work into categories (e.g., logos, brochures, websites, and so forth) in a print portfolio unless you have a similar number of pieces of work to put into each category. A portfolio should represent your skills and abilities (as a whole) rather than emphasizing the number of times you've worked in a particular medium or format. An uneven distribution of portfolio pieces might unintentionally suggest that you are stronger in one category and less so in another. In an online environment, your work has the potential to be tagged, filtered, and viewed in categories more readily. Unfortunately this option is more difficult in print mediums.

PORTFOLIO STRATEGY: Cezar Arvelo

Cezar Arvelo received his degree from Valencia College in 2012 and moved to New York to pursue a career as an illustrator and graphic designer. After living in New York for a couple of years, Cezar relocated to Los Angeles.

Q: What kind of strategies did you use when you put your portfolio together?

A: I specialize in illustrations, and illustrator jobs aren't very easy to find. I tried to make sure that I showcased my illustration skills, but I also wanted to show my versatility. I wanted to prove that I was able to create an entire brand identity because this skill set is very appealing to businesses and clients. Throughout my portfolio, I tried to show how my solutions could be extended in various mediums to give the impression about how they might play out in real life. I felt it was important to communicate to my clients and the people I interview with that I understand how business works.

Q: When I look at your work I get a graffiti, whimsical, skateboarding, culture jamming narrative. Is this accurate?

A: Yeah, those are pretty accurate. At the time graffiti was my first love, but something I didn't want to pursue as a career because it has a stigma attached to it—similar to anime. When I was in school students were given kind of general assignments to complete, and when it was time for us to put our portfolio together we were asked to take our best solutions and redo them to make them stronger or expand them further. Personally, I didn't like many of my solutions, so I decided to start over from scratch and create new projects for my portfolio. My teacher told me that this was a risky move, but he supported the decision. My goal was to create seven new pieces that I could get excited about and reflect my personality. Many of these pieces had an urban feel and allowed me to showcase my illustration skills. There were a lot of little micro-decisions that felt good about. I felt like this was a good decision because when I began interviewing for jobs, it was easier for me to sound passionate about my work.

Q: I've been told that it's important to put the type of work in your portfolio that you are passionate about doing. Do you agree?

A: Absolutely, the type of work you put into your portfolio can influence your career. It's important to edit your portfolio strategically.

Q: If you could go back in time to your senior year when you were conceptualizing your portfolio, what advice would you give?

A: I'd probably tell myself to make more meaningful work and to make sure to pay close attention to the details. I may have used a few too many shortcuts back in school, so I'd warn myself to be careful. I'd probably tell myself to focus more on the digital aspects of the game like UX/UI because the world has become digitally oriented.

Cezar Arvelo

When Good Enough Just Wasn't Good Enough

If you look back through history you can find examples of how being perceived as 'good enough' can put a bad taste in consumers' mouths. According to legend, the Gibson Guitars Corporation ran an advertising campaign in the early 1940s that seemed brilliant initially and then backfired when a competitor attempted to shape consumers' perception of Gibson's guitars as being 'adequate' rather than highly innovative musical instruments. When you read this story, think about the danger you might face if you create a safe, middle-of-the-road, portfolio instead of embracing a little risk.

....

Orville Gibson began making guitars out of a one-room workshop in Kalamazoo, Michigan and founded the Gibson Mandolin-Guitar Manufacturing Company in 1902.

Gibson made mandolins initially, but his innovative spirit led him to invent an archtop guitar, which was an acoustic guitar with a carved, undulating top similar to that of a violin. By 1930, Gibson had established itself as an innovative company that was not afraid to break away from tradition and experiment. As a result, Gibson created one of the first commercially produced hollow-body electric guitars, which made an indelible mark on the music industry.

In the early 1940s Gibson launched an advertising campaign, which declared "Only a Gibson is Good Enough" in an attempt to cap-

ture a greater share of the market and establish itself as a leader in the industry. In fact, the company was so happy with their campaign that they began stamping "Only a Gibson is Good Enough" on the necks of their guitars.

Epiphone, one of Gibson's main musical rivals, felt the sting of Gibson's ad campaign and responded with a strategically worded campaign of their own. Epiphone's ad simply stated, "When 'Good Enough' Just Isn't Good Enough" and used Gibson's own words against them.

Epiphone's response to Gibson's campaign was brilliant because they understood that musicians wouldn't want to spend money on a guitar that was only considered 'good enough.' Epiphone hedged its bet on the fact that artists would make their purchasing decision around 1) Perceptions of a brand and 2) How owning a particular guitar made them feel.

As you build your portfolio it's important to show that you aren't just 'good enough,' but to use this as an opportunity to show that you bring something special to the table and that you have a unique skill set.

4. Creating Your Narrative

Your portfolio should craft an experience for viewers, where your attitudes, abilities, brand, passions, and personality are interwoven into the content. Your portfolio is a visual extension of you and requires you to find an angle (a thing, a concept, a twist, a hook, etc.) that makes you stand out from the crowd.

The ability to make your portfolio look prominent is paramount, and the last thing you want to do is to play it safe and create a 'good' portfolio. Instead, set your sights at creating a 'great' portfolio. There are lots of good portfolios out there and positioning yourself in the middle of the pack is a quick way to get nowhere fast. There's too much on the line to play it safe and conservative. The middle of the pack is filled with ultimately forgettable portfolios, lacking focus, relevance, confidence, energy, and passion. Worse yet, reviewing an uninspired portfolio can often feel like a big waste of time.

Nobody gets excited about investing in something that is perceived as being 'good enough,' but people get downright enthusiastic and excited about spending time and money on things that make them feel awesome, unique, or empowered. I can tell you from first-hand experience, an employer won't get excited about hiring a candidate who is 'capable,' but they will be downright ecstatic about hiring a motivated candidate who is eager to roll up his/her sleeves and contribute.

When I hire an employee, I don't want someone who duplicates the skill sets of my current team. My ideal candidate is someone whose skill sets complement those of my team, meets my most immediate needs, and adds another dimension to the list of services that I can offer my clients. Metaphorically speaking, if I already have a hammer in my toolbox, I can almost guarantee the next tool I purchase will be something other than a hammer. Consider how your training, experience, talents, and qualities make you unique. It's exceedingly likely that your journey, experience, and reasons for choosing your profession is different from those of your peers—even though you probably share similar interests. You and your classmates may have similar academic experiences, but what is it that makes you unique? It can be a hard question to answer without spending time thinking about it, but its implications can be meaningful.

As you prepare your portfolio and begin thinking about your work you'll need to select pieces that are unique and highlight your best qualities. Work that demonstrates your experiences and skills are relevant, as well as work that supports your narrative and expresses your passion. Imbuing these messages into your portfolio is similar to how a gem cutter cuts facets in a diamond to reflect the light in such a way that the gemstone looks immaculate and magnificent. Your portfolio can be so much more than just providing samples of your work. It can represent your skills, growth, decision-making process, personality, work ethic, problem-solving abilities, and the list goes on.

Trying to communicate all of your positive qualities isn't a good idea because it can look braggadocious, but strategically focusing on some of your better qualities (especially those the employer is looking for) is a good strategy.

IDENTIFYING YOUR STRENGTHS

The question you need to wrestle with is how you can take your interests, skills, and personal qualities and weave them together to create a narrative that aligns with the needs of the employer? For example, if the position you want to apply for requires you to work on a team, it might be a good idea to include a portfolio piece demonstrating how you've contributed to the success of a group project in the past. Essentially, you're identifying an employer's need and addressing it through the curation of your portfolio. If the position requires the candidate to possess a heightened attention to detail, then it might be a good idea to give the craftsmanship of your portfolio a similar level of scrutiny. Once you define the message of your narrative you can reinforce these messages in the design and construction of your portfolio.

You might find it helpful to refer to the paper you wrote and reread your article again with this question in mind. "What qualities should you try to communicate through the curation, construction, and design of your visual portfolio?"

Questions You Might Be Able to Address Visually in Your Portfolio

The following questions are based on a conversation with Cinnamon Pritchard, VP, Executive Creative Director for Pace Communications, located in Greensboro, NC. As you read through the list, think about ways you could address these questions in your work to make your portfolio stand out.

. . . .

01. Do you have experience working in a team-based environment? What role did you play and how do you credit other team members?

02. How are you creative outside of work? What inspires you to be creative in and outside of work?

03. What's your creative process like? What steps do you take before attempting to solve a problem? What is your insight for whom your solution is targeted for?

04. What evidence do you have to show how you have dealt with constraints? How do you deal with constraints that you may not personally agree with?

05. What is your work ethic, personality, and sense of humor like? Are you hip and cool?

06. Do you use analytics, polls, or other data to help you make the right design decisions for your target audience?

07. Do you know enough about the medium you are working in to know what's possible? Do you know enough to push the envelope or make good decisions?

08. Have you thought about where the piece in your portfolio goes next? What's the next step you'd take if you were asked to continue developing the piece further?

09. Have you given yourself any self-imposed challenges? What risks have you taken in your solution?

10. How long does it typically take you to complete a portfolio-worthy solution? You might have a semester to finish a piece in school, but could you do it in a week?

11. Are you aware of current trends in your profession? What tools, trends, and insights are you familiar with?

The narrative of your portfolio is one of your biggest gambles.

You can communicate a lot about yourself through your portfolio and in many cases visual evidence trumps talking about these qualities in yourself. Imagine you are hiring for position requiring candidates to possess a critical eye and consistent attention to detail. One candidate says, "I have a keen eye for detail," and the other candidate says something similar, but then opens his portfolio and shows examples of his work which demonstrates his accuracy and impeccable eye for detail. Which candidate do you think made the stronger impression? Most people would agree that the candidate who showed examples of his critical eye and attention to detail will have made the biggest impression.

The trick to creating a strong narrative is to consider how each element in your portfolio reinforces and works with the others. Think about the different types of decisions you can make with regard to your portfolio.

PORTFOLIO VARIABLES YOU CAN MANIPULATE
- Number of pieces, quality of work, and the curation of your portfolio.
- Order in which you display the work in your portfolio.
- Layout, design, and typography and grid system.
- Type of portfolio, construction, and craftsmanship.
- Your brand elements and visual identity.
- Photographic, illustrated, and written content.
- Your overall consistency, flow, and pacing.

The key is to make good detail-oriented decisions and then stepping back to look at them from a macro-view when putting your portfolio together. The narrative you imbue in your portfolio is one of your biggest gambles you'll make. It's a superb idea to get feedback from others about what your portfolio should communicate, but ultimately you need to take ownership of the narrative since you'll be the one rolling the dice.

In a nutshell, you are wagering that the narratives you include in your portfolio will appeal to a hiring manager. There's always a risk that this message will miss its mark, so it's important that you are the person making the strategic decisions along the way. Getting feedback from others you trust during this time can help you feel more at ease with the decisions you make.

PROJECT ANALYSIS: What's being communicated?

Mitch McRee created a hauntingly beautiful and macabre wine label for his portfolio. Mitch described the wine as "copious amount of black cherry flavor, complemented by notes of black-berry with a hint of licorice. It's a bold fruit flavor countered with a tinge of dark chocolate."

Mitch commented, "I created the illustration by using charcoal and coffee to draw the picture" and the name 'Double-Take' references the type of reaction I wanted customers to have when seeing the bottle on the shelf or tasting the wine for the first time.

One thing is sure, Mitch's carnival-like, freak show style of illustration paired with a retro hand drawn typeface visually sets the stage for a unique wine tasting experience.

A CONVERSATION WITH MITCH

Q: Why did you create the Double-Take wine piece for your portfolio?

A: The main reason I created this piece was to show off my illustration and typography skills. The majority of my artwork is hand drawn illustrations that I do for fun, and I wanted to bring some of this artwork into my design portfolio. I feel like this example sets the tone for the other elements in the label.

Q: What kinds of thoughts were going through your mind when you created this solution?

A: A lot of my artwork themes are dark, and I was reading a bunch of horror stories (like H.P. Lovecraft) at this time. I also watched a season of American Horror story about a freak show circus which probably also influenced my design decisions. My goal was to create a wine label that would challenge my audience to participate in thinking of an occasion to consume this wine. If I saw wine like this on the shelf, I'd buy it just because the label is different.

Q: **Did you consider how your concept could be extended into other mediums (e.g., wine box, coasters, advertising campaign, etc.)?**

A: I didn't think about a wine box, but I thought briefly about coasters before deciding that they were probably more oriented toward beer. I wanted to design the cork for this piece, and I had thought about creating a motif with trapeze artists on it to continue my creepy carnival theme. I also considered a balancing wine rack, etched with a laser cutter, but I was pressed for time and didn't have a chance to extend the portfolio piece beyond the wine label.

Q: **How does this piece tie into other pieces in your portfolio?**

A: I feel like it fits in with some of the darker pieces in my portfolio, but I also wanted to show some of my versatility and range. The piece ties in with my background in hand drawn illustrations and introduces the viewer to some of my favorite color combinations that I use in other places in my portfolio. It's one of my stronger pieces and shows up first in my portfolio. I feel like it's representative of my interests and design abilities.

BREAKDOWN

· This piece demonstrates Mitch's illustration skills in a design context. Clients often have tight budgets and may be unable to afford to hire an illustrator. Mitch's illustration skills may be regarded as an asset by a hiring manager.

· Mitch's use of nontraditional mediums (e.g., charcoal and coffee) is noteworthy. A hiring manager might interpret this small detail as an example of Mitch's ability to challenge the status quo and look for alternative solutions.

· Mitch demonstrates that he understands what elements are required on a wine label. He has included details like wine type, date, volume (mL), the percentage of alcohol, website address, government warnings, and a UPC label. This information shows his design solution is strong enough to support these elements.

· Mitch's typefaces seem well chosen, but how well he handles his typography is unclear because the label is predominately image driven. A Creative Director or Hiring Manager will probably look at other pieces to determine Mitch's typographic abilities.

· The most unfavorable comment that Mitch might receive about this portfolio piece is that he missed an opportunity to demonstrate how he might extend the project. For example, Mitch might want to consider developing an advertising campaign, website, point-of-purchase advertising, or other marketing materials. Adding items such as these demonstrates that Mitch has the ability to see beyond the problem in front of him and that he thinks about how a brand or project could be extended further.

DEFINING YOUR STRATEGY

Refer to the paper you wrote earlier and the notes you took during your interviews. What things do you need to include in your portfolio to make it appeal to your audience? The first step is to have a brain dump and list as many attributes, qualities, or considerations that you can. The second step is to sort back through your list and prioritize these items.

Use this list to emphasize the most important considerations and to remind yourself to look for opportunities to neutralize these concerns in your portfolio. Take a look at the example below and then list the attributes, qualities, or considerations important for you to address in your portfolio.

PORTFOLIO CONSIDERATION	RANK
EXAMPLE: I was told that it's important for the work in my portfolio to be consistent. I need to look out for design elements (like my color system, typography, or grid system) that might give me trouble and identify ways to manage these aspects better. For example, I can download and install Adobe Capture on my mobile phone to capture colors from an image to speed up and improve my color picking skills.	☆ ☆ ☆ ☆
	☆ ☆ ☆ ☆
	☆ ☆ ☆ ☆
	☆ ☆ ☆ ☆
	☆ ☆ ☆ ☆
	☆ ☆ ☆ ☆
	☆ ☆ ☆ ☆

REFLECT, PRIORITIZE, STRATEGIZE

"The best thing for my creative process is a deadline."
—Jeff MacNelly

5. Budgets, Deadlines, and Feedback

By now you should have a firm grasp on your audience, their needs, and the narrative of your portfolio. The last bit of planning revolves around logistical needs like setting a budget, establishing a timeline, and gathering feedback.

The Senior year is the time when students wrap their head around the scope of the work they need to complete before they graduate and begin putting together a plan to achieve these goals. The best place to begin is establishing a realistic timeline and a list of items you'll need to complete to make your transition from an academic to a professional environment as seamless as possible.

There's an adage that states, "The only way to eat an elephant is one bite at a time." Building your portfolio is a big task, but you should find some comfort in the fact that not everything needs to be done at once. Hopefully having a plan in place will make you feel more comfortable with the work you need to do.

SETTING DEADLINES

Backward planning is a method of planning where you start by identifying the outcomes or goals and then you work backward to space out and set deadlines. The typical college semester is about 15 weeks long, so to begin setting deadlines for yourself you need to decide what you want to accomplish in this time. Your professor may have specific goals (and deadlines) for you, so if this is the case, then your next step should be to talk to him or her about the course requirements. If you are working through this book independently, or if your professor is willing to be flexible and set deadlines and goals with you, then your first step needs to be identifying what your scope of work looks like. Determining the scope of work is important because it allows you to allocate the right amount of work and resources to complete the project on time.

> *"Creating a 9 piece portfolio (especially when 6 out of 9 pieces are new projects) is a big task, but breaking this process down into smaller parts makes the project more manageable."*

When I teach my senior-level capstone class I require students to complete the following tasks over a 15-week period:

- Create a nine-piece (minimum) portfolio
- Participate in a mock interview
- Attend a portfolio review
- Create a print and digital résumé
- Write a six- to eight-page research paper
- Complete a freelance assignment
- Establish a monthly budget and record three months of data

This scope of work is ambitious, but my students are given the details about the assignments on the first day of class. We spend some time discussing how these tasks can be broken down into smaller, more manageable parts, and what the deadlines will be. For instance, the job of creating a nine-piece portfolio can be broken down further into a series of scaffolding steps with opportunities for feedback along the way.

- Three Pieces: Go through your entire body of work that you've produced and pick your three best and applicable pieces. Rework them, so they are portfolio quality and support your narrative.
- Six Pieces: Create three new portfolio pieces that will appeal to your target audience and take portfolio quality photographs of all six of your portfolio pieces (be sure to shoot establishing shots and detail shots of interesting areas).
- Nine Pieces: Create three more portfolio pieces, one of which should include a freelance project or project that you are particularly passionate about, photograph these three pieces and write titles and short descriptions for all your pieces.
- Final Portfolio: Work on the layout, branding, and construction of your professional portfolio. All of your work and craftsmanship should be immaculate.

Creating a nine-piece portfolio (especially when six out of nine pieces are new projects) is a big task, but breaking this process down into smaller, more manageable parts makes the task a bit easier. As a rule of thumb, most students can create three new portfolio pieces in a three-week period, but it can be an intense experience.

Divide and Conquer Your Portfolio by Load Balancing Your Efforts

You are probably beginning to get a sense of how many pieces you are going to put into your portfolio and it might be a good time to hit pause in order to think about balancing your workload. Every semester I see my seniors attack their workload in the first half of the semester only to run out of gas during the second half of the semester—if only there was a better way!

Welcome to my quick introductory to load balancing your efforts. As you make decisions about how many projects you need to create, break these projects down into even smaller parts to get a sense of how complicated or involved they will be.

It will feel great to rework a few of the design solutions you created in your classes because they can usually be modified quickly since you aren't starting from scratch. However, it's the new portfolio pieces you are going to create that may slow your pace down.

As such, it might be helpful to load balance your efforts by beginning to think about which pieces you can work on together in order to speed the process up. For example, if one of the projects in your portfolio is a logo for a beer company, a business card, a packaging design solution, and a social media campaign, most people would consider that a fairly involved project. It might be a better strategy to schedule a less time consuming project to work on in order to balance the load.

Additionally, breaking projects down into smaller parts can help you make better decisions with regard to your time, stress levels, workflow, and resources. If you have two projects that require you to screenprint, then work on these pieces simultaneously to save time. The planning stage is where you want to think about where to strategically invest your energy and resources.

ESTABLISHING YOUR SCOPE OF WORK

Maybe a nine-piece portfolio is appropriate for you too. Or perhaps you'd feel more comfortable creating a 12-piece portfolio and having the ability to switch a few projects in and out. Or perhaps the number of pieces in your portfolio has already been determined for you. A common request of many graduate school applications is to submit a 20-piece portfolio, and when a specific number of portfolio pieces are specified—it's a good idea to adhere to this constraint.

Establishing the scope of your project up front can be a pain, but it often winds up being a time saver in the end. The plan you identify needs to be flexible enough to deal with unexpected events but structured enough to help hold you accountable for your time and establish clear deadlines.

PROJECTS YOU CREATED IN SCHOOL

Including a few portfolio pieces from school provides you with an opportunity to talk about your academic experiences in an interview. Most hiring managers are aware that young professionals are likely to have academic work in their portfolios, so you shouldn't feel self-conscious about not having an abundance of professional experience. That said, hiring managers still want to see examples of work that's relevant to the position you are applying for. The work you put together during your academic career needs to be balanced with projects you create to help position yourself as a good candidate for the position you want.

You might be asking yourself, "Why can't I make a portfolio out of the work I already have?" to which I would reply "You can. Well, kind of..."

You might not realize it, but professors sometimes recycle projects from year-to-year because a project is effective at teaching a particular lesson. This recycling of projects often makes many student portfolios look almost identical and ultimately forgettable. Remember how we touched on how important it is for you to stand out earlier? Well, projects that get often recycled present two problems: 1) they aren't likely to help you stand out and 2) if a hiring manager has already seen this type of project before they mentally begin comparing your work to the other solutions they've seen in the past.

I remember going to a job interview early in my career, and the art director who was interviewing me looked at my portfolio and said, "Oh, I see you had Professor Mc-Cullough. I remember doing this same project for him when I was in his class. Not much has changed, since I've been there has it?"

Immediately the art director began to mentally compare my brochure to every other brochure he had seen over the last 15 years. Talk about pressure! I didn't end up getting

PROJECT REVIEW SHEET

It can be extremely helpful to go through your entire body of work and think about what pieces you might want to rework in order to make them portfolio pieces. The chart below can be filled out and help you make decisions more quickly.

Project Name	Category	Medium	Date	Description
Example: Internet ad campaign	Advertising	Digital	April 2016	A series of three advertisements for Clorox bleach. The three ads use animated gifs.

> *"It's perfectly fine to have a few portfolio piece from your academic career, but you miss out on an opportunity if you only include portfolio pieces from your academic experience."*

the job, but when I returned home I removed the brochure from my portfolio and began working on a replacement piece immediately.

In my opinion, it's perfectly fine to have a few portfolio pieces from your academic career, but you miss out on an opportunity if you only include portfolio pieces from your academic experience. Not only is there more to your story than your academic accomplishments, but your portfolio narrative may adopt an 'assigned projects' theme that can sometimes feel disconnected from your personality and passions. For this reason, I think it's a smart decision to add new, inspired work to your portfolio.

LEARNING TO WORK EFFICIENTLY

One of the most valuable resources you have to account for is time. I find it helpful to print out a calendar and type in deadlines, important dates, reminders, and notes. I also find it useful to enter my deadlines on my Google calendar, so I can look them up quickly using my laptop and smartphone. However, creating a physical calendar first helps me better identify where the demands for my time are likely to be.

When you are setting up a timeline, it's typically not a good idea to try and manage one project from start to finish before starting the next. It's much more efficient to multitask instead. For instance, if I find myself waiting for feedback or making printing arrangements, then I'll start working on the next project until I resolve what I was waiting for initially. You may find it helpful to have a project 'on deck' so you don't find yourself sitting around waiting for feedback, a shipment to arrive, or a file to come back from the printer. Not only is this an efficient use of time, but it's fairly representative of what you can expect when you transition to a professional environment. If you've been fortunate enough to work on one project at a time, then multitasking will be a good skill for you to practice. If you are still developing your multitasking skills, then here are a few steps you can take to make multitasking easier.

Clearly define your tasks: Define your tasks in advance and decide on a distinct set of tasks that you are going to complete and stick to them! If you think of an additional task, then put it on a list to work on at a later time.

FEBRUARY

Sunday	Monday	Tuesday	Wednesday	Thursday	Friday	Saturday
			1	2 Begin working on my résumé / Bring in body of work to discuss during class crit / Begin keeping a monthly budget	3 Begin reworking 3 favorite pieces	4
5	6	7 Rough draft of research paper is due. Print out for crit	8	9 Begin looking for a freelance client to work with	10	11
12 Finalize first three portfolio pieces	13 Get reworked piece printed and mocked up	14 My first three portfolio pieces are due / Next 3 portfolio pieces due / Research paper (final) is due	15 Begin working on ideas for the next 3 portfolio pieces	16 Talk to teacher about ideas and get feedback	17	18
19	20 Begin taking photos of my work / Look into Photoshop mock-ups	21	22	23 Rough draft of résumé is due.	24	25
26	27	28 Finish résumé critique during class				

IMPORTANT DATES

FEB 7: Rough draft of research paper due. Have printouts for class critique
FEB 9: Freelance project assigned. The first half is due March 14th
FEB 14: 6–8 page research paper is due!
FEB 14: First three portfolio pieces are due!
FEB 23: Rough draft of résumé is due!
MAR 2: Bring in monthly budget to class to show the teacher.

NOTES TO MYSELF

Research paper is worth 15% of final grade!

Put deadlines, important dates, reminders, notes, and other commitments down in physical form so you can make realistic goals. Small goals are important to have so you feel like you are accomplishing things and it may help motivate you to keep going.

Group compatible tasks together: It's smart to pick tasks that can be worked on at the same time. If you have to photograph a portfolio project, then there might be an advantage to shooting several of your projects at the same time. Photographing multiple projects at once will reduce your equipment setup and breakdown time, you might be able to batch edit your images in Photoshop, and it may be easier to arrange for someone to assist you for a two-hour photography session rather than making arrangements for three separate 40-minute photography sessions.

Take advantage of downtime: Let's face it, the world isn't going to stop while you put your portfolio together. The chances are good there will be other demands on your time. Get into the habit of bringing a sketchbook and a pen with you and if you find yourself waiting around for another project, then fill the void by working on one of your smaller tasks. It's a good idea to sketch out all your concepts before you begin working on the computer, so fill gaps in your schedule with ideation, process work, and refining your thoughts. You might be surprised to find that you can fill up a sketchbook quickly once you get into the habit. If you can chip away at a problem little by little it adds up over time. Save the smaller things on your to-do list to work on at times when you know you won't be as productive.

Create a To-Do List: When you're multitasking, sometimes it's hard to see the big picture. Putting together a to-do list can help you remember what needs to get done and when. Don't rely on multitasking to solve all your time management issues, but it can be a great tool to help you boost your efficiency. As you complete items on your to-do list mark them off and move any remaining items to the top of your to-do list for the following day and begin your day right where you left off.

Sometimes you just can't multitask: Sometimes multitasking just isn't a time saver, it becomes more of a distraction. It's important to know when a project requires your complete attention. When this happens there's not much to do other than roll up your sleeves and grind it out. While multitasking can make you more efficient overall, occasionally you may need to stop multitasking to stay focused on a particularly complex task.

Eliminate known distractions: One of the biggest distractions I see capturing my student's attention regularly is email, instant messenger, and social media. If you want to multitask efficiently then allowing known distractions to continue is a bad idea. Chances are good that you do your best work when you're focused and engaged, so don't be afraid to unplug and turn off distractions when you need to make the best use of your time.

LEAVING TIME FOR EXPERIMENTATION, FEEDBACK, AND CRAFTSMANSHIP

To save time and maximize their efficiency many students often compress and underestimate the amount of time needed for experimentation, craftsmanship, and critique feedback. If your plan your timeline around the amount of time it takes you to complete a project on your computer, chances are good that the solution won't be as fully developed as it could be otherwise.

While saving time and maximizing your efforts is a worthy endeavor, it can't come at the expense of the quality of your design solution. As a general rule plan on spending between 20 and 33% of your time wrestling with, and understanding the problem better, exploring it from various angles, and developing possible design solutions. Similarly, take the time to test your solution and receive feedback about its potential strengths and weaknesses. I usually try to leave around 10 to 15% of my projected time spent on

Leaving yourself time for good craftsmanship allows you to recover when/if you run into an unexpected problem. This piece titled The Nutcracker Sweet ran into unexpected printing issue that needed a little extra time to be resolved.

a project to plan for and gather feedback and make adjustments to my solution. Getting feedback on a project you're invested in can be emotionally difficult, but as you already know, it's important to keep an open mind.

One area I see students occasionally underestimate is how much time it will take to print and mock up their work. We've talked about the importance of establishing a narrative in your portfolio, but if part of your story is built upon the idea that you 'pay close attention to details,' then your craftsmanship is a critical step in reinforcing this message. Attention to details is a must in every portfolio.

Paying attention to the small details encompasses not only spelling and grammar, but control over your printing and fabrication methods as well. Craftsmanship issues usually occur when we feel rushed and pressured to finish quickly. Leaving a little extra time at the end of a project can help if you hit an unexpected snag.

I created the promotional piece titled, The Nutcracker Sweet (above), to send to my clients for the holiday season. I wanted to keep the cost of the project down, so I printed out my design on cardstock using a color laser printer. The printouts looked great, and I was pleased with how vibrant the design looked on the page.

My next step was to take the printouts and cut out the box design from the cardstock using a laser cutter. Cutting the boxes out with a laser cutter allowed me to cut out the box design quickly and accurately, and since I had access to a laser cutter it was simply an investment of time rather than money.

After spending the better part of an afternoon cutting out my boxes, I returned home to fold, glue, and assemble them. As soon as I folded the first box, I noticed that the toner on the edges had begun to flake off. By the time the boxes reached my clients, I feared it was going to look even worse. I quickly folded together another box to double-check the results and the same thing happened again. I knew I needed to make adjustments because poor craftsmanship wasn't a message I wanted to deliver to my clients.

I retraced my steps and trying to understand what was making the toner flake off guessed that the toner wasn't being fused to the paper because the fuser wasn't getting the cardstock paper hot enough to properly fuse the toner to the paper. As soon as I folded the second box, I watched the toner chip off again right before my eyes. I thought to myself, "What am I going to do? How can I fix this?"

I liked the weight of the cardstock and I didn't want to switch to a lighter weight of paper, so I decided to experiment with different ways to print my design and used an inkjet printer instead of a laser printer. I was worried my design wouldn't look as vivid and bright on an inkjet printer, but I knew the paper would absorb the ink down into the fibers of the paper instead of having the toner sit on the surface of the paper.

I printed off a test print and waited for it to dry. When it was dry I folded the cardstock anxiously waiting for the results. The inkjet print held up nicely, so I reprinted my files, recut, and assembled the boxes again.

All in all, I lost about 24 hours of time, but I felt it was a necessary step to keep my holiday message focused on goodwill—not poor craftsmanship.

It can be challenging to work with a material, process, or tool you aren't familiar with…especially when your timeline is tight. If you find yourself treading into unknown territory—good for you! But it's probably a good idea to build a little extra time into your schedule to experiment, fail, learn from your mistakes, and recover.

DETERMINING YOUR BUDGET

Most students don't have unlimited funds to spend creating a portfolio, and the price of a portfolio can range anywhere from $50 to $500. Generally speaking, the more work you're willing to do yourself the lower your price will be. You can get a wooden cigar box for around $2.00 and convert it into an impressive portfolio with a little elbow grease. Alternatively, you can purchase a custom-built 11" x 17" portfolio by kdbooks.com or kloportfolios.com for around $180.00 to $210.00. These companies build custom portfolios for their clients and can help reduce your portfolio construction time and help you avoid issues with craftsmanship.

While some people may view a $200 portfolio as a good investment if it helps get them a good job, others may have a more modest budget to work with. As you continue to prepare and complete work for your portfolio, you're likely to face this and other expenses. Planning how to use your financial resources is another step in the portfolio creation process. You will also need to factor in printing costs, mock-ups, props and backgrounds for photography, artwork and stock photography, fonts, hardware and software, and other items. That $200 you have to spend on a portfolio might look more like $450 by the time all of these other expenses are calculated into the equation.

> *"A ream of high quality résumé paper might cost around $15 for 500 sheets and $45 for 500 envelopes. If you split your order with a classmate then your expenses will drop dramatically."*

Aside from budgeting wisely and picking up a few extra hours at work, there are a number of ways you can save yourself a few dollars.

Shop around: Before you make a purchase check for reviews, competitor advertisements and prices, and coupons. Websites like camelcamelcamel.com allow you to see how prices on Amazon.com have fluctuated and set up an alert when items on your wish list have price drops. A Google Chrome application like Honey will automatically try to apply various coupons during checkout to save you extra money. There's nothing wrong with being frugal and trying to get the most bang for your buck!

Order samples: Before you go to press or purchase specialty items order samples first. For example, paper representatives are usually more than willing to send you a swatchbook or few sheets of a specialty paper to let you see how the paper looks before requiring you to purchase a larger quantity. Similarly, many printers have print samples they can send you so you can see how certain printing techniques and materials will look before placing your order. Samples are usually free, although you might be charged a shipping fee for expedited shipping.

Work together: Talk to your classmates and set up a Facebook group for your class to see if anyone wants to split a paper order or other supplies with you. A pack of waterslide decal transfer paper might cost around $20 for ten sheets, but most students don't need more than a sheet or two. If you split the order with your peers, you might only end up spending $4.00 (especially if a member of your group has free Amazon Prime shipping). A ream of high-quality résumé paper might cost around $15 for 500 sheets and $45 for 500 envelopes, but if you split your order with a classmate, then your expenses may drop dramatically.

Stock photography: While this tip isn't really about saving money as much as helping you spend it more wisely, before you pay for stock photography image you might want to check to see if the image you're considering is overused. Simply download the thumbnail

PROJECT EXPENSE SHEET: Fill one sheet for each portfolio piece.

PROJECT NAME	EXPENSES

PROJECT ELEMENTS
- ☐ Artwork or Illustration
- ☐ Stock photography
- ☐ High-resolution scans
- ☐ Specialty paper/material
- ☐ Envelopes

- ☐ Fonts
- ☐ _____
- ☐ _____
- ☐ _____
- ☐ _____

MOCK-UP EXPENSES
- ☐ Digital mock-ups
- ☐ Screen printing
- ☐ Adhesive material
- ☐ X-acto knife and blades
- ☐ Mounting expenses

- ☐ Printing costs and supplies
- ☐ Other tools or items
- ☐ _____
- ☐ _____
- ☐ _____

PHOTOGRAPHY
- ☐ Background element
- ☐ Camera/lens expense
- ☐ Lighting equipment
- ☐ Film/memory card
- ☐ Location rental fee

- ☐ Model fees
- ☐ _____
- ☐ _____
- ☐ _____
- ☐ _____

OTHER RELATED EXPENSES
- ☐ Domain name
- ☐ Web hosting plan
- ☐ Hardware expenses
- ☐ Software expenses
- ☐ Storage/archive fees
- ☐ Matchprint or other proof

- ☐ Travel expense (gas, hotel, etc.)
- ☐ Shipping expense
- ☐ Equipment rental
- ☐ Competition fees
- ☐ _____
- ☐ _____

ESTIMATED TOTAL

from the stock photography website and go to images.google.com and do a reverse image lookup. If you discover the image has been used too many times, you might want to consider purchasing a different image instead.

Buy in bulk: Buying in bulk is a way for you to drop your per unit price. For example, if you know that it's likely you'll go through lots of X-acto blades when mocking up your work, then you might want to consider purchasing a box of 100 blades for $18.00 instead of a box of 5 blades for $3.99. Even though the price of the bulk package of 100 blades is more expensive purchase initially, each blade ends up costing $.18 compared to $.80 per blade when purchased as a package of five. A sharp X-acto knife blade is worth its weight in gold when it comes to cutting your work neatly, and you'll end up saving money over time. It may also be worth mentioning that you can also resharpen an X-acto blade with fine grit sand paper to extend their life a little longer.

Shop local: Talk to local vendors to see if they would be willing to offer your class a small discount for using their services. You might be surprised to see how easily you are offered a 5–15% discount on products and services. Talk to your classmates and decide which local vendors you are likely to use. The more people in your class who agree to use a particular vendor's services, the more incentivization the vendor will have to offer you a discount. It may also be worth checking if any products or services are available through your academic institution. Many academic programs offer students a great rate on printing through a print services facility. While they might not be able to turn work around very quickly, they can often offer students discounted prices. Your university may offer a similar service, so make sure to ask around and explore what options are available before you go out and pay retail prices.

Student discounts: Even if you need to make a retail purchase, take a moment to ask if the company offers any kind of student discount. Student discounts aren't just for entertainment and retail purchases, but you can find numerous technology, software, travel, tickets and admission, shipping, and other products and services. There's no shame in asking about discounts, and the worst that can happen is to be told: "No, we don't offer a student discount."

GETTING FEEDBACK BEFORE MAKING BIG PURCHASES
Before you pull out your wallet and make a big purchase, take a little time to get some feedback on your concept or idea. Take it from someone who's learned the hard way,

Gather feedback before spending a significant amount of money.

making purchases before you've worked out the details can cost you extra time and money. The act of explaining your idea to someone who isn't invested in it can sometimes open up new directions to explore, more efficient methods of working, and better allocations of your resources. They may point out a more efficient workflow, allow you to borrow or trade for the items you need (rather than purchasing them), help you identify a lower-cost alternative, or assist in discovering a method for reducing the price.

While it's important to experiment, most of us need to pay attention to the budget. Like many things in life, striking a balance is key, and if you find a way to save money then I encourage you to take advantage of it. Relying on a friend to sound off your ideas can help you quickly identify the holes in your plan and ground your ideas in reality.

A few years ago I created a branding system for myself and spent $400 to get a custom-printed, embossed, foil stamp made. The stamp turned out beautifully, and I was excited to start using them. The only problem was I didn't spend enough time figuring out how I would incorporate the stamp into my letterhead and collateral materials. I was so focused and enthralled with making the stamp that I lost focus on its purpose. If I had only taken a moment to just get a little feedback I could have saved myself a last-minute letterhead redesign. I'm quite certain I would have been asked, "Have you mocked up the stamp on some of your letterhead yet?" and I would have realized that I was so enamored with the foil stamp that I had lost sight of my end goal.

Falling in love with the idea of exploring a medium, technology, methodology, or technique is not the end of the world, but critiques can help ground our explorations in purpose—just in case we lose sight of our goal. It's a good idea to talk with someone you trust about your concept before making any kind of significant financial investments. The act of explaining your idea to someone else can help confirm that you are heading in the good direction and also reveal where the weaknesses in your plan lie.

GETTING CONSTRUCTIVE CRITICISM HELPS
An important aspect of creating a killer portfolio is taking the time to gather feedback on your projects along the way. Listening to how others perceive your work is a critical aspect of the design process, but getting good feedback and responding to constructive criticism isn't always easy.

The first step in gathering feedback is identifying periods of time where getting feedback is helpful. If you are working on a 9-piece portfolio, then getting feedback three times is probably sufficient, but you'll need to look for different types of feedback each time. For example, you might plan to receive feedback after you've completed your first three portfolio pieces to reaffirm that the quality of your portfolio pieces is at an appro-

> *"When you get feedback on your portfolio, your job is to stop talking and start listening. Resist the urge to interrupt, explain, and defend your decisions."*

priate level. More specifically, you might look for feedback about the quality and appropriateness of your work, the depth of each project, and consensus about whether your projects are likely to appeal to your target audience.

After you've completed the first six portfolio pieces, you might ask for feedback about whether a theme or narrative is beginning to emerge, any perceived strengths or weaknesses, and if any craftsmanship or presentation issues are present. Once you've finished all nine portfolio pieces, you'll probably want feedback about the scope of your work, the pacing of your portfolio, how it's viewed as a collection, and help identifying any outliers which don't seem to fit your narrative.

It can be tough to divorce yourself from your work—especially when you are being graded and trying so hard to make a good impression. Getting feedback isn't always fun, but this is why scheduling feedback sessions ahead of time can be helpful. It creates a chance to stop and take a moment to look at your work through someone else's eyes.

When you get feedback on your portfolio, your job is to stop talking and start listening. Resist the urge to interrupt, explain, and defend your decisions. Remind yourself they are reacting to the work that's in front of them—not critiquing you. Just because someone doesn't agree with a decision you've made doesn't make your decision wrong, but it's important to try and understand what made them feel that way. Try (even though it may be difficult) to have a thankful attitude and an "I appreciate your insights" tone during your critique.

If you receive feedback that you don't agree with or don't understand, then you should discuss this with your professor or peers in order to better understand the issue(s). Receiving negative feedback can be a bummer, but it's part of the refinement process and a perfectly normal part of the design process. Your work will be stronger if you listen to how it's being perceived and address these concerns. The worst thing you can do is to ignore the feedback you receive and resist changing anything because it's inconvenient for you.

Your portfolio is a living document, and while you might not receive an adverse comment on a piece during the first or second round of feedback, you might receive negative feedback later in the process. I've had students hit the roof when one of their first three portfolio pieces received negative feedback in a later round of critiques.

"They've seen this piece twice and only had nice things to say about it. Why are my reviewers giving me negative feedback on it now?!" my student exclaimed. I had to explain in the context of three portfolio pieces the solution worked fine, but in the context of a nine-piece portfolio the piece no longer held its weight.

I explained to my teary-eyed student this was a good thing because the quality of her portfolio had obviously gone up, and the audience's expectations of what to expect from such a talented student had gone up too. I remember the student's tears drying up fairly quickly after looking at her negative comments this way. You simply have to roll with the punches and be open to input from others. If you keep an open mind and positive attitude, you're likely to end up in a really good spot.

CHAPTER REFLECTION

A strategic plan helps you work more efficiently by helping you decide where to invest your resources. You can run out of money, time, and other resources quickly if you don't plan ahead. Taking inventory of what you've already accomplished, what you still need to do, and mapping out your time helps you make better decisions along the way. Leaving time to gather feedback is a way of reaffirming your choices.

Getting feedback on your work can be painful, but not getting feedback on your work can be costly. While getting negative feedback is never easy it can help you ground your efforts in reality, which is often sorely needed. Sometimes we often get so caught up working on a project that we lose sight of our goals and what messages are being communicated.

You can still expect to run into obstacles and roadblocks along the way as you begin working on the projects that will go into your portfolio, but hopefully, the number of obstacles you encounter will be drastically reduced.

ACTIONABLE ITEMS

- ☐ Defining your portfolio strategy. Determine what messages are the most important to deliver to your audience.
- ☐ Complete a student project review sheet and identify which projects you might want to retool for your portfolio.
- ☐ Create a timeline (with deadlines) for your portfolio. Leave yourself time to gather feedback and make adjustments.
- ☐ Fill out a project expense sheet for each project in order to estimate your budget.

6. What to Put in Your Portfolio

As you prepare the body of work to include in your portfolio you need to make sure you've got your bases covered. As a rule of thumb, you shouldn't put work into your portfolio that you don't want to do professionally. If you dislike website design, then don't put website design work in your portfolio. Your portfolio needs to communicate the things you are passionate about, engaged with, and interested in. It seems so obvious, but often students feel pressured to include certain types of projects in their portfolio.

Mary Struble created the package design solution on the opposite page during her senior year at Virginia Tech. Mary comments,

> When I created this piece I was pretty new at packaging design, so I did a lot of research to figure out who my target audience was and what type of company would create this type of solution. I determined that a solution like this would be created by a hot sauce enthusiast who would do all the packaging themselves and cater to a niche market. In my mind, it's a smaller company who has a sense of humor and knows their literary references.
>
> I did a lot of research on Dante's Inferno and that's really what I used to anchor my concept. Hot sauce is spicy, and Dante's Inferno had multiple levels of hell, which I translated to levels of heat in the hot sauce that get progressively hotter. Each level of hot sauce is named after that level of hell starting with Limbo and ending with Treachery. On the back of the label I included a quote from the literary work that states, "Abandon all hope, ye who enter here," which is something Dante says before he enters hell.
>
> For me, the most fun part of this project was creating the labels because I purchased some canvas and pulled it apart, wrapped the top of the bottle with twine, used a lighter to singe the labels—giving them a charred, burned feel. I almost destroyed my inkjet printer in the process. I ended up using a canvas that wasn't meant to go through inkjet printers and some

A detail shot of Mary's Dante's Inferno hot sauce.

of the threads got caught on my printer and got caught. I swear my printer is still spitting out bits of canvas to this day! It ended up being a really great project, but I really tried to make it a project that was anchored in research, rather than a piece that was simply designed to look cool. I think this has stuck with me because grounding my concepts in research is something I try to do with all my work, even to this day.

As you can see with Mary's piece, the examples of the work you put into your portfolio can really help you tell a story. Simply put, your work is the main ingredient and the other elements in your portfolio should help support and complement this work.

Your work should be relevant to the position you're seeking, unique, and showcase your ability to control the design principles to tell a story. From Mary's decision to use an industrial looking, condensed sans serif typeface, to the dramatic use of lighting in her photograph, to her research into Dante's Inferno, her solution is both eye catching and well controlled. Take a look at Mary's solution again with these thoughts in mind:

- **Conventions:** You can tell that Mary looked other hot sauces and thought about what content was necessary for her to include. Information like nutritional content, UPC code, and fluid ounces is typically required on products that are sold in stores. Often these are elements that are left off by less experienced designers who tend to focus only on the aesthetics rather than addressing how a packaging needs to function.
- **Scale and Proportion:** Mary repurposes a Tabasco bottle, which is a brand of hot sauce many people are familiar with. Ideally, her hot sauce solution would have a unique bottle shape (and cap) of its own.
- **Hierarchy:** The name of the hot sauce company, 'Dante's Inferno' is the most visually dominant element on the label because of its scale, color, and capitalization. This is followed by the flavor of the hot sauce—indicated by a number and its name. Tertiary information, like the ingredients and UPC code, is treated as supporting elements. This makes sense with regard to typical consumer purchasing priorities.
- **Texture and Material:** Part of what makes this piece stand out as being a creative piece is how Mary used a burlap-like material for her label and twine around the neck of the bottle. The frayed edges of the material make us feel like the hot sauce is so spicy the label can barely hold on! Additionally, the label may trigger a memory of fire hoses firemen use to extinguish fires, which conceptually links us to a tactile experience we may have had at some point. Inviting users to have a tactile experience with a hot sauce is a unique and creative approach to serving up an experience to consumers. The burlap material gives the impression that this hot sauce isn't made in bulk by a molecular gastronomist in New York, but rather someone who makes hot sauce regularly as a part of their tradition, culture, and heritage.
- **Photography:** The establishing shot is symmetrical and static, while the detail shot is asymmetrical and dynamic. As you begin thinking about photographing the work in your portfolio, remember to take numerous shots (40+) with variations in lighting, composition, and proximity to the object. By using a camera lens with a shallow depth of field the photographer, David Mudre, keeps the audience's attention focused on the label design and away from details in the background that might become distracting

elements if they were in focus. The audience's eyes move from the bottles to the light source in the right-hand side, then they return and settle on the center bottle, moving to the green arrow, and up to the 'Abandon all hope' text.

Mary's design solution and the photography is creative and well controlled. Mary's design can be extended to various flavors of hot sauce. If she wanted to extend the project, then she might consider creating a series of magazine advertisements, point of purchase displays, or billboards. Mary's solution is memorable, shows a sense of humor, and demonstrates her control over various design principles. This piece has the potential to be used as an opening portfolio piece and helps set the tone for Mary's portfolio. The piece is upbeat and creative. Branding and packaging hot sauce look like a fun project to work on and will appeal to many audiences. You may want to exercise caution if you are considering using a wine or beer label as the opening piece in your portfolio. Generally speaking this would be a perfectly acceptable portfolio piece, but you might want to establish a rapport with your audience through the other pieces in your portfolio first.

> *"It's important to begin your portfolio with a very strong opening piece in order to make a good first impression."*

Mara Frontera's menu (shown on the opposite page) demonstrates her understanding of hierarchy, color, and unity. Her menu is photo dominant on the front, and typographically dominant on the back. On the front of the menu Mara makes good use of the photographs and chose images to highlight the fresh ingredients used at the restaurant. Mara creates a sense of energy through the use of diagonal lines, and uses these lines to pull the viewers eye's down toward the name of the restaurant at the bottom. On the back side of the menu Mara uses a simple, yet contemporary, sans serif typeface that is easy to read and uses typographic weight and color to establish typographic hierarchy.

Mara's design isn't overly complicated, but it's a solid solution. The textures and background help the viewer establish a sense of scale and set a tone for how the menu design would look in a high-end environment. Mara extended this piece in her portfolio by designing a signage system for the restaurant. When Mara showed her design to Taaza they asked her to use her menu design in their restaurant and wanted to hire her to redesign their website as well.

This opportunity gives Mara a positive narrative to work into her portfolio. What initially started as a concept piece was shown to the restaurant and as a result they asked

The Taaza, Fresh Indian Bistro menu was designed by Mara Frontera.

to hire her to design their menu and website. It's a great narrative and one that demonstrates how Mara's design project was successful! This confirmation helps validate Mara's concept and design decisions and demonstrates how she can solve problems and create opportunities.

When you present work in your portfolio, it's likely that your solution will be critiqued on your ability to use the principles of design effectively. An Art Director will look at your use of balance, emphasis, movement, pattern, repetition, proportion, rhythm, variety, unity, contrast, and alignment and determine how well you control the design principles. As they continue to look at your work they will evaluate your conceptual abilities, typography, grid system, calls to action, how effectively you communicated your message, and other elements. When you think about the steps you take to visually solve a problem, you might use a design process something like:

· **Understand the problem:** You might be given (or asked to write) a creative brief; you might take notes and have discussions about your client's goals and the needs of the target audience; or you might be asked to work around a particular set of constraints.

> *"Showing your research, sketches, or how your concepts evolve might be a good angle for you to show how your design and/or thought process is unique."*

- **Research the problem:** You might conduct a field study; look up examples of precedence on the Internet, investigate the topic on various social media platforms, go to the library and look through publications; or create a series of iterative thumbnail sketches.
- **Brainstorming:** You might develop a word list; use one of your favorite design methodologies; create a series of rough sketches; or put together a mood board.
- **Design:** In the design phase you typically develop tight sketches, computer renderings, mock-ups, and prototypes.
- **Presenting work:** When you finish your solution you typically present your work to your family, friends, colleagues, clients, art director, professor, and so forth. You might discuss your point of departure, research, concept, design decisions, medium, and any feedback you've collected. You might ask for additional insights and use the information to test your design solution before finalizing it.
- **Production:** When you reach the production phase you often shift your focus to touchpoints, developing mechanicals, getting files ready for print or coding.
- **Assess:** After the work has been completed you may revisit the creative brief again and determine how well you met the goals of the project, conduct meetings to help facilitate the roll out, and establish and/or collect metrics to evaluate your solution's success.

When you created your design solutions maybe you didn't use all of these steps, or perhaps you used steps that aren't listed above. It might be advantageous to show how your design solution evolved or how well it was received by your audience. If you include some of this information and additional insight as part of your visual portfolio, it can help make a good design solution look even more impressive because it roots your solution in communication, problem-solving, and understanding. Often the behind-the-scenes glimpses are a part of your process that employers are interested in seeing, but less likely to see.

Think back to an earlier chapter where we discussed the importance of standing out from other designers and creating a narrative for yourself. Showing your research, sketches, or how your concepts evolve might be a good angle for you to show how your design and/or thought process is unique. Keep this in mind as you create new projects

SHOW THEM HOW YOU GOT THERE

> *"Even if the position you identified in your research paper is a specialized position, your portfolio should show a range of work."*

for your portfolio. You might want to sketch with a pencil or pen on a paper that will be easy to scan, take a copious amount of notes, use a particular design methodology, or keep track of data to show how your design solution generated a particular response.

You shouldn't feel like you need to show your process work for every project in your portfolio, but being able to show how you arrived at a particular design solution a few times can be incredibly helpful and extremely interesting to discuss in an interview.

I've had students express that they felt their sketches and process work weren't at a level they felt comfortable including in their visual portfolio. I can sympathize with these sentiments because I don't feel my sketches are beautiful either. To be fair my sketches we never created to be beautiful, but they were created to help me develop a concept or resolve a problem. My sketches aren't at the same visual quality as the other work I put into my portfolio, so I put my sketches into a sketchbook and bring it with me instead. When it's advantageous to show my process work I pull out my sketchbook and share my sketches. I consider my sketchbook to be more of a supporting document rather than trying to integrate it into my portfolio because it makes me feel more comfortable to present my work this way.

I've worked with students like Elizabeth Zimmerman and others whose sketchbooks are a thing of beauty. If my sketchbooks looked like Elizabeth's I would totally integrate my sketches into my portfolio. Unfortunately, my process work is much more unrefined, so carrying a sketchbook to accompany my portfolio is preferable to me. There are a lot of strategies for showing your research, sketches, and other components, so find the solution that works best for you and make sure you save all your sketches, process work, and data from here on out!

WHEN TO EXTEND A PROJECT

If the job you want to go into is a specialized position, your portfolio should show a range of work. Even if you want to go into web design, then you'll probably want to show more than websites in your portfolio. You might want to think about including projects like ad banners, blogs, brand identity, electronic newsletters, investor relation materials, logo designs, micro websites, motion graphics, a press or media kit, social media promo-

Peacock House
Bed & Breakfast

history:

Built in 1860 by captain William Trott
Decorated in Federal & Revivalist styles
Passed to the Peacock family in 1880
 when Robert Peacock married the
 captain's daughter
Main part of the house redesigned in 1896
Renovated in 1988 after neglect, opened
 as a B&B with 20 rooms

LUBEC, ME

The easternmost town in the U.S.
creative arts hotspot
outdoor activities - cycling, hiking,
 beaches, lighthouses, birding,
 whale, seal + puffin watching
 fishing, hunting, boating
Bridge to campobello island, canada

SPECS:

- cheapest room: $115, most expensive: $165
- 7 bedrooms with private baths
- Full breakfast in A.M.
- Library + gathering room w/
  piano, sun room, fireplace
- garden & porch

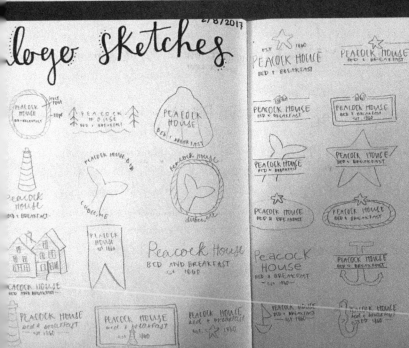

Two pages from Elizabeth Zimmerman's sketchbook.

tions, and so forth. While your portfolio will feature website design, some of the other projects listed above may be relevant to the scope of work that a web designer may be asked to work on. If you were to create nine websites for your portfolio—and that's the only type of work you show in your portfolio—you risk pigeonholing yourself and your websites might begin to compete with each other. By folding other (related) work into your portfolio you diversify your portfolio, demonstrating the range of your abilities, and reducing competition between the pieces in your portfolio.

On the opposite page I've put together a list of different types of projects to help 'prime the pump' with regard to how you might 1) extend projects and 2) identify types of projects that might be relevant to the position you want to obtain. When you read the list, keep in mind the narrative you're trying to communicate about yourself through your portfolio. Some projects may be relevant to your ideal job, while others may be less so. Talk to others about where you're likely to get the most bang for the buck.

Sometimes it's necessary to extend a project in order to make the scale of a project seem more significant. For example, if you designed a logo for a florist, then you might want to show more than just the logo for the florist in your portfolio. You might want to consider designing a vehicle wrap, business cards and letterhead, a brochure, an advertisement, or a social media campaign too.

Extending a project might not be terribly important if you show your process work and design methodology leading up to your final solution, but if you aren't feeling super confident about the strength of your process work, or if it's in a format that makes it difficult to include in your portfolio, then extending the project might be a good idea.

When you extend a project it's important to show how your design decisions translate to other formats and mediums. Don't just duplicate your efforts in a superficial way—it might backfire and look like you got lazy and took a shortcut.

Shelby Baitsholts created a lovely typographic logo for herself. However, sometimes a logo can seem small or insignificant if it's displayed by itself. This requires that you either show an ample amount of sketching, your design process, or extend the project in order to make it seem larger. Mocking up a logo on a business card and letterhead is perfectly fine but if a logo is extended in other ways that demonstrate its range and versatility, it is likely to be perceived as being a more substantial solution. Shelby's logo is a strong logo, but she's fighting against the perception that it is simple and didn't take

Types of Projects to Consider Incorporating Into Your Portfolio

Ad banner	Guerilla marketing	Point-of-purchase display
Advertising campaign	Hang tag	Postcard
Analytics overview	Illustration	Poster
Annual report	Infographic	Public Service Announcement
Apparel	Information sheets	Presentation
Augmented reality	Instagram campaign	Press kit
Billboard	Interactive campaign	Print ad
Blog	Interface design	Proposal
Book cover	Internet commercial	Radio advertisement
Book design	Investor materials	Radio spot
Brand identity	Invitation to an event	Responsive design
Brochure	Invoice and legal forms	Sales kit
Business card	Kiosk design	Self-promotion piece
Campaign	Label design	Signage
Card	Landing page for website	Social media campaign
Catalog	Letterhead	Social media posts
Collateral material	Logo design	Social networking
Copywriting	Magazine	Sound design
Corporate event	Magazine ad	Standards manual
Digital billboard	Marketing campaign	Stationery
Digital publication	Mass transit advertisement	Sticker
Direct mail	Menu	Table tent
Direct marketing	Micro website	T-shirt design
Editorial spread	Mobile application	Television advertisement
E-newsletter	Mobile interaction	Trade show booth
Email signature	Motion graphics	Uniform
Email campaign	Movie trailer	Vehicle advertisement
Employee relation materials	Music video	Vehicle wrap
Environmental graphics	Newsletter	Video editing
Facebook page	Newspaper ad	Wayfinding system
Feature article	Outdoor board	Website
Game	Packaging	Window display
Greeting card	Photography	

An example of a lovely typographic logo by Shelby Baitsholts.

too much time to complete. Anyone who has tried to create a logo for themselves knows that this isn't always an easy process, but the rigor and methodology that Shelby used to create her logo isn't being communicated clearly. Solutions that are perceived as being 'simple' or 'easy' may need additional components to make the work seem more substantial. Celebrated graphic designer Paul Rand once said, "Design can be art. Design can be aesthetics. Design is so simple, that's why it is so complicated."

Shelby's logo is arguably a strong solution where its strength lies in its simplicity, but she needs to consider how her audience will react if the logo is shown in isolation. This is the reason why logos are often shown mocked up on business cards, stationery, store front signage, vehicle wraps, marketing collateral, leave behind items, and so forth. Showing a logo in these formats is considered the true test for how well a logo functions and also makes the work seem more significant.

If you receive comment on a project in your portfolio to 'extend your project' or to 'make it seem more significant,' then think about adding additional elements to the piece. I've had students create a poster for a ballet recital or play, and I've asked them to extend the project to make the work appear more compelling. Typically, students design tickets, play bills, or promotional items which help make the work seem more momentous.

CONSIDERING THE TRANSITION BETWEEN YOUR PIECES

As you create a body of work for your portfolio the process may be a bit more fluid than you'd expect. You'll need to be conscious of the order that work appears in your portfolio and make sure your projects transition smoothly from one to another. Emily Carlin created the two posters (on the opposite page) and used a mock-up to display the posters in her portfolio.

Emily made a good decision to change the background color of the two mock-ups and repeated some of the colors found in each of her posters. However, the aqua-colored

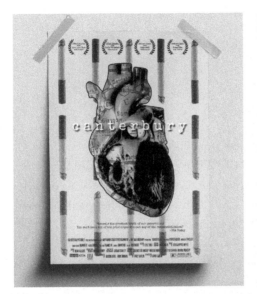 

Two posters by Emily Carlin from the University of South Alabama.

tape at the top and strong shadow makes the audience aware that the same mock-up has been used and isn't an visual element that you'd typically want your audience to be aware of. Emily must have intuitively noticed the similarity and reacted to it because she separated these pieces in her portfolio so they wouldn't appear one after the other.

Emily comments, "I wanted to incorporate the colors in the pieces into the background of the poster, but I forgot to change the color of the tape if I'm being completely honest. When you stare at something for so long you tend to miss these kinds of little details and it can be helpful to have another pair of eyes look at your work in order to catch little details like this."

Emily makes a great point about having someone you trust look at your work from time to time. These moments provide you with an opportunity to test your transitions as well as getting feedback on how others experience your portfolio.

When you are writing an essay, good transitions help connect your paragraphs and create a unified whole. Each of the pieces in your portfolio should function similarly by working together, referencing one another, and helping develop an overarching narrative. When you write you often pick up key phrases from the previous paragraph and highlight them in the following paragraph to create a progression of thoughts for your readers. Similarly, picking up concepts and visual elements from one portfolio piece and incorporating or building upon them in the next piece can help your work appear as a progression of your narrative.

On the opposite page you will find two pieces from Haley Longbottom's portfolio. The top image is an infographic she created for CRISPR, a genome editing tool that could transform the field of biology, and a package design and brand identity for Alma organic milk. Haley's organic milk solution follows the CRISPR infographic in her portfolio, but stop for a moment and consider the transition between these two pieces.

Haley's decisions to take a flat, two-dimensional solution and display it in a three-dimensional environment help ease the transition from the infographic to the Alma organic milk solution that follows. Similar to how there are many ways to create hierarchy (weight, color, scale, and so forth) there are many ways to control transitions from one portfolio piece to another. Haley comments, "These were two of my favorite pieces and I put them in the back of my portfolio to leave the audience with a strong impression of my abilities. Just like the end of firework show at the Fourth of July, I wanted to end my portfolio with some of my strongest pieces to help my audience remember me. Both of these pieces have a health-related connection (CRISPR with their DNA analysis and organic milk being a healthier option), but I really wanted to leave my audience with a strong, positive idea of my range and abilities."

Haley's solution also relies upon visual elements to help transition between the pieces in her portfolio, but other methods work equally well. For example, you could also create a transition through intellectual similarity, media, audience, function, and other criteria. You don't have to use the same transitional element between all the pieces in your portfolio, in fact, you can use variation to help build interest. Haley made a decision to give her infographic an environment in which to live, and to apply two lighting effects to the piece to make it appear more lifelike. Haley created the illusion of an infographic having a glossy surface and created a shadow underneath the infographic to create a surface.

Your transitions don't have to be obvious, but they need to be considered. I recently worked with a student on a mobile app and a print magazine spread. Neither of the pieces shared a common aesthetic, medium, or audience, but both of the pieces were similar thematically. The pieces were designed for nonprofit companies that promoted gender and sexuality issues—a topic of interest to the student. It made sense to put these pieces close to each other in her portfolio because the topic was similar and doing so provided

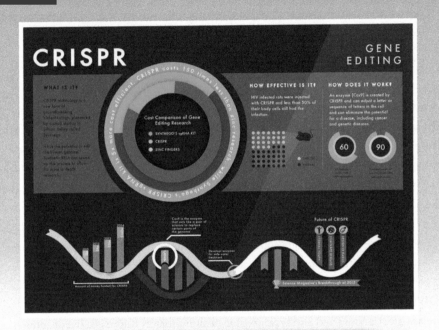

> *"You don't have to use the same transitional element between all the pieces in your portfolio, in fact, you can use variation to help build interest."*

an opportunity to work the pieces into her narrative more easily. On the flip side of the coin, I advised a student who had created several logos to space them out in her portfolio because they shared too many similarities and the logos competed with each other.

As you create the body of work for your portfolio it's important to think about how each piece will react to the piece before it and after it as well as how the piece connects to the narrative that you strategically chose for yourself. The goal is to have each piece transition smoothly and support any overarching goals for your portfolio. With a little practice your presentation will become seamless and demonstrate how well-prepared and skilled you are for the position you are applying for.

SHOWING NONTRADITIONAL CREATIVE WORK

There are a variety of tried and true graphic design projects (there is a list of some of these types of projects on page 73), but sometimes it can be advantageous to break out of stereotypical design projects. Nontraditional work gives you an opportunity to highlight your originality and ability to break away from established practices. Nontraditional work gives you an opportunity to custom-build a narrative that is unique to you and demonstrate that you can leverage your visual skills to solve problems and communicate effectively. Nontraditional creative work can be virtually anything that recontextualizes how we think about art and design, unfamiliar processes or mediums, or innovative approaches to problem-solving. In many cases a designer will fold their graphic design skills with another discipline and the results can often be unexpected and surprising.

Chris Hatfield describes his approach to design as "Being independent of a particular medium and a set of problem-solving skills, and a way of thinking, to move something from its current state to its desired state." Chris quickly credited Dave Mason, the principal at Multiple in Chicago, Illinois for helping articulate his approach to design so concisely.

It's clear that this definition of design impacted Chris because if you look through Chris' portfolio his work ranges from light-paintings to more 'traditional' design work. Chris goes on to comment, "All of those skillsets, the branding, packaging, the narrative of a piece—that's where I got to have fun and bring all my tools to table. Students today are digital natives, but what they might feel uncertain about is how to tell a story from

WHAT ARE YOU COMMUNICATING THROUGH YOUR PORTFOLIO PROJECTS? THE TIP OF THE ICEBERG OR SOMETHING MORE?

01. **DESIGN AESTHETIC**

02. **CRAFTSMANSHIP**

03. **PRESENTATION**

04. **CONCEPT**

05. **CREATIVITY**

06. **COMMUNICATION**

07. **AUDIENCE NEEDS**

08. **PROJECT GOALS AND CONSTRAINTS**

09. **ANALYSIS & SYNTHESIS OF YOUR IDEAS**

10. **RESEARCH & PROCESS WORK**

11. **PROBLEM-SOLVING ABILITIES**

12. **EMPATHY**

beginning to end—or to think of it as an evolving story. From Squarespace to hand-coding a site, designers today can pop up an online store in a weekend, brand it, package and screen print it, and ship it out."

Chris' senior thesis and the work began as part of an internship at a shop called Madhouse in Toledo, Ohio where he was doing a lot of video and motion graphics and he discovered he needed to learn Cinema 4D. Chris worked late and started watching tutorial videos and ended up tying this into his thesis work where he investigated glitches by creating demands on hardware and software and pressing them further than they were designed to go. Chris describes his results as "creating digital breakdowns where for a split second you see the intention of the user and the failure of a complex system. I was fascinated that I could produce an artifact in real time of this breakdown. So I spent a large part of my summer investigating metamorphosis, the presentations of power, and what happens when we lost control."

Chris' real breakthrough came when he stopped looking for these elements in digital form, but began seeing these qualities in his hometown community of Toledo, Ohio. Chris states,

> Toledo, has gone through some hard times and I grew up in this area. When I was around 16 years old I started playing in bands and by 21 years old I got signed and toured all over the country for a long time. I lived out in Los Angeles, California for a while and when I returned a lot of the kids I had known growing up were in positions of leadership where they are working with arts communities and museums, trying to change the culture of a city that had been struggling. There was a lot of fallout in this city where entire downtown blocks were vacant and buildings were in a state of disrepair.
>
> If you were to drive through some of the neighborhoods who were effected by racism in the past you'd find many abandoned homes in what used to be the big, beautiful, old Victorian styled homes where the executives and CEOs used to live. This changed due to a number of reasons like "white flight" and the cultural makeup of the city changing. When you add new people from different backgrounds into an area where predominantly one culture had lived—and who may have been afraid of these changes—they simply left. There's a historic legacy of redlining (to refuse to loan or insure someone because they live in an area deemed to be a poor financial risk) that has been successfully proven and sued against banks and lenders in this neighborhood.
>
> To me, when you look around this area you're looking at the latent impact of a system that has completely failed—the system is supposed to work a certain way, but doesn't. And I felt like I needed to do something and I truly believe design is a change agent. I believe when you take your thoughts, your passions, and skills, and apply them to a problem, you can make

a difference—and that brought me to creating Brick x Brick. [Brick x Brick raises proceeds from the sale of the limited edition design artifacts to benefit community initiatives working to combat the impact of poverty, inequality, and blight.]

Toledo has reinvented itself through the work of designers, artists, museums and non-profit companies in this community. Our downtown is undergoing an incredible resurgence where local boutique storefronts, large corporations, public art and murals flourish again. I'm trying to make sure we keep parts of our city included in the wealth cycle of this resurgence by supporting the leaders who have been here fighting for their homes and families the entire time. The first edition of Brick x Brick raised $1500 for a neighborhood association, and that led to my next edition. Invision App has partnered with me to release an (already) sold out edition which will trigger an incredible donation for Toledo.

A project that simply started as an investigation of glitches in software and hardware systems evolved into a project that embraced social, cultural, and political themes. Chris' project transcended the typical mediums that a design solution might typically take and he began using the bricks from dilapidated houses to screen print his message on and sell to raise money to help address a problem in his community. Chris comments, "If you're not pissed off, or elated, or passionate about your work. If you don't love something so much you feel like you need to tell everyone you know about it, or you don't hate something so much that you have to fight it—if there's nothing that you feel this way about, then you aren't showing your perspective."

Nontraditional work gives you an opportunity to tell a story or make a connection that's unique and meaningful to you. In many cases, nontraditional work gives your audience a glimpse into who you are as a person, the type of issues you care about, and who you are as a designer. In many cases, nontraditional work establishes your ability to problem-solve with inventive processes and methods, less traditional mediums, and more personal topics.

Graphic designer and illustrator Bizhan Khodabandeh initiated a comic project with cocreator James Moffitt called *The Little Red Fish*, which he was motivated to explore by an increased interest of middle-eastern political history as a college student involved in the antiwar movement during the Iraq war. Bizhan comments, "I've been doing self-initiated projects for a while now. I started out screen printing and designing my own t-shirts and ended up branching out to work on skateboard designs." I asked Bizhan how his graphic novel and other nontraditional work has been received, he replied,

Any creative endeavor in general is enriched by pursuing other interests—not just being a passive consumer. To be clear, I'm not just talking about other creative, but things like

The graphic novel 'The Little Red Fish' was written by James Moffitt and illustrated by Bizhan Khodabandeh.

athletics and other areas as well. A friend of mine and I train in Muay Thai boxing, and that particular sport incorporates pattern recognition, spotting tells, and other small details. A lot of design is about social and visual pattern recognition as well as being obsessed with details; so this sport tends toward using many of the same skill sets as a designer.

With regards to the graphic novel you're referring to, I often hear that I get hired because of my illustration skills and putting myself out there in a different way it has almost become more of a marketing element for me. I feel like I get hired even when there are some really talented designers vying for a job is because my portfolio shows a range of my skills from sculpture to graphic design. I feel like having a diverse portfolio has helped me get more jobs because it shows that I can do a lot of things and sometimes a client might only want an

illustration now, but they have another need coming down the pipe and want to establish a
relationship with someone long-term who can communicate in lots of mediums. It also helps
because not every client can afford to hire a photographer, illustrator, and graphic designer, so
having a diverse portfolio allows me to present myself as more of a one-stop shop.

What makes Bizhan's work unique is that it is clearly linked to his personal narrative, interests, and hobbies. One of the things I find most interesting is how Bizhan has leveraged his wide range of skills (from sculpture to traditional design work) as a means of differentiating himself from the competition, but also as a way to establish long-term relationships with his clients. His graphic novel, *The Little Red Fish,* started as a way for him to talk about middle-eastern politics, but blossomed into an illustration skill set that's highly valued and sought after by his clients.

DISPLAYING RESEARCH AND TRADITIONAL ACADEMIC WORK

Should you show research and other academic work in your portfolio? As mentioned before, this book is written from a graphic design perspective but the discussion can be leveraged by students from a variety of majors. If you are majoring in a discipline where research and academic work is typically seen in a portfolio, then it's imperative that you include portfolio pieces that address this need too. However, the answer to this question isn't so obvious for your discipline, you might be wondering what you should do.

The question about whether to show your research and academic work in your portfolio reminds me of another contested question within the graphic design profession, "Do graphic designers need to learn to code?" The best response to this question that I've seen came from Jim Webb in an online course called *Coding for Designers,* a course he developed for Aquent. Jim polled a group of graphic designers and found they were almost evenly split with their answers to the question, "Do designers need to learn to code?" Jim decided to poll hiring managers instead of designers and discovered that there was no consensus among this group either, meaning the answer to the question was, "It depends on the needs of the person who's doing the hiring."

"It depends" is also the answer to "Should you show research and other academic work in your portfolio?" and can only be answered by understanding the needs of your audience. If seeing your research and academic work is important to either you or the hiring manager, then put your research and academic work in your portfolio. Otherwise, leave research and academic work out of your visual portfolio.

As Jim Webb discovered, there are lots of opinions about "Do graphic designers need to code?" and the best option was to make this call on a case-by-case basis. If you feel

"IT'S NOT WORK, IT'S MY PASSION"

Swallowtail wine labels by Alex Voss while at the University of Missouri, Columbia.

unsure how a hiring manager will react to research or academic work, then you might want to either leave this work out or 'package' your research as a portfolio piece. I've had students creatively 'package' a white paper they wrote by using their paper as the content for a magazine they designed and included their writing samples into their portfolio this way. If you are unsure whether your research methods and academic work will appeal to your target audience then packaging your work this way can be a clever way to cover your bases.

INCORPORATING PASSION PROJECTS

One of the biggest messages your portfolio needs to communicate is what kind of work are you passionate about? What gets you excited? What do you enjoy using your talents for? Simply put, "What do you love to do?" The answer to this question is probably a bit different for everyone, but it couldn't be more important to answer via the work you put into your portfolio.

If the work you put into your portfolio doesn't feel inspired, or completed with a spirit of curiosity, enthusiasm, and vigor, then why would you include it? Most people can spot a fake easily, so it's incredibly important to bring a certain amount of honesty and enthusiasm to the table. Alex comments,

Detail shots of the Swallowtail wine label.

This project was one of the last projects we worked on in a packaging class and I really wanted to push the boundaries. I experimented a lot with photography and typography on this project and was really happy with how the piece turned out. The name of the vineyard is Swallowtail, which I think most people would interpret as a type of butterfly, but I chose to take it in the direction of a snake eating its tail (the symbol of Ouroboros), which is said to have connotations of infinity or wholeness. My take on the vineyard was that it was more of a hippie, relaxed vineyard. I think this is one of the strongest pieces in my portfolio because I took the project further than I had to.

Alex said he was encouraged by his professor Jean Brueggenjohann to take his own photographs, both in how he created the photographs for his labels (shown above) and how he staged the bottles for his portfolio. Alex says, "I felt it was important to my concept not to mock up the wine bottles using a stock photography template—it would have fought against my concept. When I began interviewing for jobs after college I received numerous comments about how impressed people were that I staged and photographed my portfolio pieces myself."

> *"Students often have a difficult time talking about their work on interviews...projects [you] are interested in are much easier to discuss because [you] have thought a lot about the work."*

Alex's aesthetic for Swallowtail is based on an earthy, easy-going, casual concept. His concept juxtaposes the pretentious, boutique, and highly selective culture of other vineyards. As a result, Alex's concept looks like it could be enjoyed right out of the bottle with close friends on a warm summer day. Photographing the work on orchard grass brings these sentiments home wonderfully.

Alex's professor Jean Brueggenjohann adds, "In the class where Alex created his Swallowtail wine labels I require my students to take their own photographs, make their own illustrations—everything needs to be done by them—so their pieces are totally theirs. It's a big job, but it makes a big impression." Jean says that she requires her students to come up with and pitch three concepts to her with goals that are important to the student and "want my students to be able to incorporate their voice in their project."

In a portfolio when you are trying to articulate your message clearly, it's important to have good control over all your elements. Personal expression, self-initiated projects, and projects that resonate with you personally can help remind you why you love the discipline you're trying to break into. Jean says, "My advice to getting the best work from my students is to be honest with them and give them lots of feedback to help them ground their ideas in reality." Sometimes my advice is "If you don't love what you're doing, then you need to start over. If you don't love what your solution, then it's going to show." It's hard to fake enthusiasm, and it's important that the work in your portfolio reflects your confidence and a certain energy level for your work. Jean goes on to add, "Students often have a difficult time talking about their work on interviews. I have had several student write me after they graduated and have jobs tell me that projects they were heavily invested in were much easier to extemporaneously discuss in interviews. They feel more confident to speak because they have concrete reasons for their decisions because they have thought a lot about the work."

CHAPTER REFLECTION

The work you include in your portfolio needs to be strategically chosen to not only be relevant to the job you are applying for, but to reflect your passions as well. When choosing what work to put into your portfolio, consider how your target audience will react and go beyond student-focused considerations like, "Did this project get a good grade?" or "Did this project get professionally printed?" These considerations are rooted in a student-centered mind-set and may not give your audience the right impression.

When you produce work for your portfolio it may be advantageous to show your research, brainstorming, process work, sketches, and other elements. Collect these artifacts along the way and archive them in a way that they can be shown in either your portfolio or as a companion piece to your portfolio (e.g., a sketchbook).

You might need to extend certain projects you created to make them feel more prominent or significant. As you build your portfolio it's important to think about the transition between pieces. Your portfolio narrative needs to make sense and you need to consider how your body of work flows.

Some work in your portfolio may be more traditional in nature, but don't discount the value of including a nontraditional project (if appropriate to your discipline). Nontraditional portfolio pieces can be used to strategically point out your understanding for the role design can play in a political, social, or cultural context. Nontraditional work can provide you with an opportunity to show your understanding and control over the communicative power of design.

While research and traditional academic work isn't typically included in a visual portfolios, you might consider packaging your research or academic work in some cases. In disciplines where research and traditional academic work is expected, you'll need to include this information in your portfolio. In other cases, you might want to build a project around your academic work to better contextualize it within a visual portfolio.

Finally (and perhaps most importantly), it's imperative to communicate that you're passionate about your work and to highlight work that reinforces this message. While the work still needs to be relevant to the job you are applying for, work that indicates you love what you do is highly desired.

ACTIONABLE ITEMS
☐ Work on creating a body of work and take into consideration some of the topics that have been discussed in this chapter. Make sure your work communicates your passions, while continuing to be relevant to the position you are applying for.

PLAN
PLAN
PLAN
DO IT

7. Branding Yourself

The core of branding is rooted in memory and recognition, and good branding can increase the audience's perception of value. In a nutshell, branding represents the sum of the audience's perception about an organization, person, place, or thing. A brand can be used to establish an impression that doesn't necessarily have to be rooted in facts. This is an important distinction to make because students have expressed to me that they need to be 'excessively honest' with employers. Don't get me wrong, I fully support being honest with your potential employers, but I encourage my students not to build their brand around their identity as a 'student.' Instead, I try to encourage and help students strengthen their brand by choosing a more strategically chosen theme like being a 'young professional' instead.

Many students feel awkward with titles at first, and understandably so. You've spent the last several years identifying yourself as a student, and a sudden shift to young professional or other title will probably take some getting used to. I like to remind my students their academic studies have been preparing and equipping them to enter their chosen profession so the leap from 'student' to 'young professional' probably isn't such a big leap after all once you stop to think about it. However, this shift represents a massive leap forward regarding establishing your brand. Employers aren't looking for students, they're looking for employees. Students get offered internships, while young professionals get offered jobs. Which of these directions sounds better to you?

Just to be clear, 'young professional' might not be the term or branding strategy that's best for you—I'm just saying I'm 99% sure that reinforcing you're a recent graduate probably isn't your best option. A branding strategy that looks a little less student-like and one that is more professional is likely to be a better option. Perhaps there's a particular skill you possess that's in demand, you might choose to incorporate elements into your brand. For example, students who have both HTML and CSS experience might consider having some subtle coding elements in their brand identity. For instance, you might choose some of these digital qualities to influence your typographic choices.

If your audience discovers that part of your skill set is revealed as a subtle component of your brand visuals, your branding system will appear even more rich, communicative, and hopefully elicit a positive reaction in your audience. Positive reactions to your work are what you're after, and when you produce more positive reactions than the other candidates you are likely to end up getting a job offer.

BRANDING HELPS ESTABLISH TRUST AND CREDIBILITY

Having a professional appearance helps you build credibility and confidence, while an inconsistency diminishes it. Employers need to be able to trust their employees, and having a professional looking brand is a subtle way to communicate that a company can put their trust in you. A good brand strategy can help you look polished and legitimate (even if you may not feel this way on the inside) and increase your audience's perceptions of your credibility. When students hear the word 'branding' they often begin thinking about logos. If part of your branding system includes a logo for yourself, then you might want to use this element to help you distance yourself from the association of being a student or recent graduate.

Recently the Association of American Colleges and Universities asked both employers and college students a series of similar questions about career preparation and found students rank themselves as being prepared in areas where employers do not.

This is particularly the case for applying knowledge and skills in real-world settings, critical thinking skills, and written and oral communication skills—areas in which fewer than three in 10 employers think that recent college graduates are well prepared. Yet even in the areas of ethical decision-making and working with others in teams, many employers do not give graduates high marks.

In a similar survey conducted by Bridge, they report there is often a perceived disparity between the skills entry-level employees need to succeed and new hires that possess those skills and are ready to hit the ground running. This survey also indicates that 85% of managers feel their organization is effective at training new employees, but pay particular attention to soft skills like teamwork, work ethic, professionalism, and critical thinking.

Fortunately, these soft skills are aspects you can address through your branding to help you create a positive reaction in the mind of the employer. When you create enough positive results through your résumé, cover letter, portfolio, and other business-related documents you stand out from the competition and create a small advantage for yourself. At each step along the way keep asking yourself, "What does my audience want/need to see?" and little by little your killer portfolio will begin to come into focus.

THINKING BRIEFLY ABOUT VERSATILITY

It's important not to jump too far ahead and start thinking about the form your identity system will take before you've fully worked out your message, but I sometimes find it helpful to take a moment to consider formats and needs briefly.

Many students choose to create a logo for themselves as an element of their brand identity. A good logo is distinctive, appropriate, communicative, and often simple, but it also needs to work in a variety of formats. *Smashing Magazine* offers five principles of effective logo design which include:

LOGO NEEDS! (handwritten)

- **Simple:** Easily recognizable with an unexpected or unique element
- **Memorable:** Easy for the audience to remember and recall the logo later
- **Timeless:** Consider how well the logo will work years from now
- **Versatile:** How does the logo work at various scales, colors, reversed out, etc.
- **Appropriate:** How well the logo 'speaks' to the intended audience

ASK THESE Qs FOR LOGO DESIGN (handwritten)

From these five principles, there's one that I believe is worth addressing in slightly more depth at this particular moment—versatility.

I often see students painstakingly struggle to create a logo they are happy with only to beat it into the ground overusing it in their portfolio, business documents, website, social media accounts, and so forth. Don't make the mistake many students make and confuse branding with repetition. A logo is one component of an identity system—not the entire identity system. An identity system consists of all of the style guidelines and frameworks to deliver a cohesive and memorable experience. A good identity system may also use color, typography, photography, illustrations, iconography, and design systems to create an emotional response.

BRANDING SYSTEM: Seungmi Kwon

CMYK
4% 76% 69% 0%

CMYK
1% 26% 99% 0%

CMYK
52% 0% 24% 0%

CMYK
78% 13% 54% 1%

CMYK
6% 4% 4% 0%

BEBAS NEUE

LOREM IPSUM DOLOR SIT AMET, CONSECTETUER
ADIPISCING ELIT, SED DIAM NONUMMY NIBH
EUISMOD TINCIDUNT UT LAOREET DOLORE MAGNA
ALIQUAM ERAT VOLUTPAT. UT WISI ENIM AD
MINIM VENIAM, QUIS NOSTRUD EXERCI TATION
ULLAMCORPER SUSCIPIT LOBORTIS NISL UT
ALIQUIP EX EA COMMODO CONSEQUAT. DUIS

ROBOTO CONDENSED LIGHT

Lorem ipsum dolor sit amet, consectetuer adipiscing elit, sed diam
nonummy nibh euismod tincidunt ut
laoreet dolore magna aliquam erat
volutpat. Ut wisi enim ad minim
veniam, quis nostrud exerci tation
ullamcorper suscipit lobortis nisl ut

TEXTURE 1

TEXTURE 2

Needless to say, while your logo may be the most identifiable element of your brand identity it shouldn't be the only part you use to create a cohesive and memorable experience for your audience. Nor should your logo be applied to every surface and page in your portfolio, business documents, website, collateral piece, and social media account. Repeat after me, "Consistency is great, but mindless repetition is bad." Developing a logo for yourself (particularly a logo you are genuinely happy with) will take some effort and brain power, but that doesn't mean that 1) the logo represents your entire brand identity or 2) your logo gives you license to put it on absolutely everything. Versatility, consistency, and cohesiveness of your brand, rather than repetition, is a goal you are trying to achieve.

CREATING A MOOD BOARD

Creating a mood board is a way for you to create a visual palette to pull from to help you establish your branding system. A good mood board will help you make design decisions more rapidly because you will have already identified and collected many of the visual elements in your system.

Details about colors, textures, patterns, shapes, typography, illustrations, and photography can be worked out before having to use these elements in your portfolio, résumé, and collateral materials. As such, it's a good idea to work on a 'focused' mood board rather than pinning hundreds of portfolio or branding photos on Pinterest.

A focused mood board is one where you've been selective and discerning about the elements you're pulling together, while always thinking about the needs of your audience and the type of message you want to communicate. It may be helpful to take some time to look outside of your discipline and consider images from architecture, biology, interior design, and so forth.

ELEMENTS TO THINK ABOUT FOR BRAND GUIDE

SO GOODY

✳ Colors

- The website *color.adobe.com* is a tool that allows you to build color profiles and connect these profiles to your Adobe Creative Cloud account. You just log into the website with your Adobe username and password and use the online tools to create analogous, monochromatic, triad, complementary, compound, shades, and custom color profiles. You can even upload a photo and have the software extrapolate the color profiles from the image. Once you're happy with a color profile, you can save it to your Adobe Library and access it through all of your Adobe Creative Cloud applications by going to Window > CC Libraries. You simply select an element on the page and click on any of your colors in your 'Color Themes' to apply the color to your elements.

Raise your right hand and repeat after me, "I promise that I won't steal, appropriate, or 'borrow' any design concepts that I didn't create myself in my professional portfolio, and I will purchase or get permission to use any fonts, photographs, and illustrations that I did not take or create myself."

YES!! GOOD RESOURCES

- The website *colourlovers.com* is a community-based resource that allows you to assemble, view, and share color palettes and patterns. I find many of the color palettes, particularly when sorted by 'most loved' and 'most favorites,' to be really useful and a great time saver.
- The website *paletton.com* is a tool that allows you to put together monochromatic, analogous, triadic, tetrad, and free-styled color systems together and allows you to see how they would look by previewing your colors in a fictitious website.

INSPO

- The website *design-seeds.com* uses photographs to create inspired color palettes that you can draw inspiration from.

Patterns
- The website *thepatternlibrary.com* is one where patterns are donated and shared by the community and are free to use in your designs. Simply go to the website and scroll down to preview their selection.
- The website *toptal.com/designers/subtlepatterns* is one where patterns are available for website backgrounds. The patterns are free to use as long as you credit the source in your HTML or CSS code. You can also use Subtle Patterns in your print projects, but

you need to make sure the resolution of the files is satisfactory before printing because the image resolution has been optimized for the web and may appear pixelated in print mediums. If the situation arises, you can download one of the back ground patterns, open the file in Photoshop, and go to Select > All. The next step is to go to Edit > Define Pattern and give your pattern a unique name. Then this seamless texture will appear when Edit > Fill and choose 'Pattern' in the Contents drop down menu to apply the pattern.

Typography

Generally speaking, most free fonts are a poor alternative to purchasing commercial fonts, but most of the students I've worked with are on a tight budget. If you're able to then please support type designers and purchase your fonts, but never steal a font. In fact, there's no need to steal your fonts when you've got some really good free options at your disposal.

If you have an Adobe Creative Cloud account then you have access to over 200+ fonts for syncing and 900+ web fonts on *typekit.com*. Simply log into Typekit with your Adobe Creative Cloud username and password. In the lower right-hand side of every font you'll either see the words 'In your plan' or 'Available to purchase.' If the font is in your plan, simply choose the typeface and click on the 'sync' button to sync that typeface to your computer to begin using it. If the font isn't in your plan you can see what it would cost to purchase that particular font.

If you don't have a Adobe Creative Cloud account, or simply want to consider more options, then *fonts.google.com* is another great resource. Google Fonts are completely free to use in both personal and professional projects and they have over 800+ fonts you can sync, use on your website, or download to your computer.

Once you have identified a font you like, simply click on it and then click on the red circle with a plus to select the font. A black bar will appear at the bottom of your web browser and when you click on the black bar options for downloading, syncing, or embedding the font in a website appear. Google has a font syncing application called SkyFonts that you can install which allows you to sync their fonts online rather than downloading them and storing them on your hard drive.

If you use Google Fonts, then you might want to know about *fontpair.co*, which is a resource to help you pair Google fonts together. You simply choose what type of font pairing you're interested in (e.g., a serif headline with a sans serif body copy) and you can quickly preview font combinations and download the font pairs. If you're not feeling confident in choosing typefaces that work well together, this can be a great tool to use.

<blockquote>
"The goal of a résumé isn't to get you a job—it's purpose is to make an impression quickly and get an interview."
</blockquote>

Good typographic decisions don't just depend on getting a copy of the font you like. As such there are numerous typographic resources, magazines, and books available. One online resource is a website called *typewolf.com* and they have numerous typographic resources available including: font recommendations, guides and learning resources, information about blogs and type foundries, inspiration, font identification guides, and typography cheat sheets.

Finally, if you're looking to purchase a typeface, you might want to begin your search at either *creativemarket.com* or *myfonts.com* because both websites routinely have sales where full typographic families are marked down to 90% off the normal sales price.

THINKING ABOUT THE RANGE OF YOUR TYPOGRAPHIC SYSTEM

When you start looking for fonts to use as part of your branding system you'll need to choose a font that complements your content. Choosing a typeface based on how it looks is only part of the equation—you will also need the typeface to display your content well across all your business documents and portfolio.

It probably comes as no surprise that you can (and should) use your typographic choices to help reinforce your messages. For example, a typeface with computer-like qualities like Maison Neue might help raise awareness of your 'coding abilities,' while a condensed sans serif typeface like Garage Gothic might suggest more blue-collar, urban sentiments. The thinking behind the development of your typographic system should not stop with 'the look you are after,' you also need to think about whether the typeface, including all its weights and glyphs, will meet your typographic needs.

When you create your résumé you'll need to create a typographic system that can be quickly and easily scanned. The goal of a résumé isn't to get you a job—it's purpose is to make an impression quickly in order to determine if you are a candidate worth interviewing. As such, you will need to choose a typeface that not only looks good, but one that allows you to create clear and distinct typographic hierarchy so your content can be digested quickly. Of course, your type also needs to function well in various different sizes, colors, and weights in order to be used successfully in all of your documents.

The best way to test your typographic hierarchy is to print out some dummy, or fake copy and make test prints from the printer you plan on using. You'll quickly discover

Test it out!

Bitter
This body copy is Raleway. One of the funny things about the stock market is that every time one person buys, another sells, and both think they are astute.

Ben Hannam
Ben Hannam is an award-winning designer, educator, author, business consultant, and small business owner. He thinks of himself as a desig... lem-solver, who believes that day problems reinforce the v... help make the world a bette...

Ben is an Associate Profes... cations at Elon University... plish Studios, LLC in orde... and to help bridge the g... graphic design professi...

Ben Hannam
Ben Hannam is an award-winning designer, educator, author, business consultant, and small business owner. He thinks of himself as a design tactician and problem-solver who believes that creative solutions to everyd... ...rce the val-ue of graphi... ...ter place.

...unications
...Studios,
...bridge
...ofession.
...rom Vir-
...Graphic

...cus
...viditib

...i

...per-
...net
...ace

Alegreya
This body copy is Source Sans Pro. One of the funny things about the stock market is that every time one person buys, another sells, and both think they are astute.

Alegreya Headline
This body copy is Open Sans. To succeed in life you need three things: a wishbone, a backbone, and a funny bone.

OPEN LEADING →

Alegreya Headline
This body copy is Source Sans Pro. I love deadlines. I like the whooshing sound they make as they fly by. Why do they call it rush hour when nothing moves?

LOVE THIS →
NICE CONTRAST

Bitter Headline
This body copy is Raleway. One of the funny things about the stock market is that every time one person buys, another sells, and both think they are astute.

Bree Headline
This body copy is Open Sans. My grandmother started walking five miles a day when she was sixty. She's ninety-seven now, and we don't know where the hell she is.

OPEN LEADING, →
REDUCE SIZE

Kreon Headline
This body copy is Ubuntu. Society is like a stew. If you don't stir it up every once in a while then a layer of scum floats to the top.

GREAT SCALE →

Merriweather Headline
This body copy is Open Sans. I've always wanted to go to Switzerland to see what their army does with those week red knives.

It's paramount to print out your text often in order to evaluate it.

that your text looks different from how it looks on your computer screen. In addition to experimenting with different typefaces, you may want to play around with your point size and leading until you reach a point where you're happy with the results.

When you print out your test prints, pay particular attention to how various weights, special characters, punctuation, and numbers look. These are often problem areas that have the potential to jam you up later.

For instance, if you have date ranges incorporated into the text of your résumé like '2016–17,' then you'll notice the date tends to stand out, as if it was written in capital letters. If you want to avoid this, then pick a typeface that has proportional old style numerals that look like '2016–17' instead. You can tell that old style numerals were designed to integrate numbers into upper and lowercase text far better than lining numerals that line up on the baseline and were designed for accounting purposes.

The version of Palatino that I'm currently using in this book doesn't have proportional old style numerals, but to use them you simply select your text and go to Window > Type and Tables > Character in Adobe InDesign, and then select the '≡' button in the upper right-hand side and choose OpenType > [Proportional Old Style].

In addition, I often use an 'en dash' between date ranges because an en dash was designed to typographically replace the word 'to.' An en dash can be typed easily by holding down the option button and simultaneously pressing the hyphen on your keyboard.

When you begin thinking about the communicative qualities of your typography, combined with typographic hierarchy and special characters, you are well on your way to making a more well-informed typographic choices. It's a good idea when you're designing your résumé and portfolio that your name is easy to find and high in terms of your typographic hierarchy. In addition, your contact information should be in close proximity to each other, making these items easy to find. Chances are good that your résumé will be broken down into sections like:

- Achievements
- Activities
- Awards & Recognitions
- Contact

- Education
- Employment
- Exhibitions
- Honors

- Leadership
- Memberships
- Relevant Experience
- Skills & Proficiencies

Under each of these sections you may have subsections or supporting information. For example, in an 'Education' section of your résumé you may also have other supporting information like: Education, Your University, Degree, Major/Minor, Date, and GPA.

In this example the 'Education' section needs to be visually emphasized, followed by the name of the school, and then the rest of the information. Take a look at the examples below and notice what information is being visually emphasized through changes in typographic weight, scale, color, and proximity. You'll notice that some of these typographic decisions make it easy for the content to be scanned quickly, while other options require a bit more effort.

EDUCATION

University Name   **Your Major, BFA**
Location   Dean's List: Dates

} The name of the university and the name of the major have the same typographic hierarchy. The use of a tab stop might make the major and supporting information difficult to scan.

EDUCATION

UNIVERSITY NAME, Location

BFA, YOUR MAJOR/MINOR

Dates, Dean's List

} The use of color interrupts the flow of the information because our eyes travel to the color first, then upward to the Education header, and finally down to the supporting information. More control is needed.

YES! TRUE

EDUCATION

University Name BFA Date
Major: Your Major/Minor
Dean's List

} The viewer suddenly becomes aware of the dotted line because of the addition of color. The color and lack of punctuation in the content needs to be addressed.

EDUCATION
University Name
    Bachelor of Fine Arts: Major/Minor
    Expected Graduation: Year
    Dean's List, Date

} The addition of color to the header will make the sections easy to scan, but this trick won't work with every color. In addition, the .25 inch tab stops make the supporting information difficult to scan quickly and disrupts the left-hand side alignment.

EDUCATION

University Name   BFA in Major, Date
Minor
Dean's List

A clear typographic hierarchy has been established, but how well this information flows remains to be seen. This concept depends upon how well this system can be extended to other sections on the résumé as well as other documents.

EDUCATION   **University Name**
BFA in Major, Date
Minor, Dean's List

A solid typographic solution that doesn't rely on color, but once again consistency over time will determine how successful this typographic solution is.

EDUCATION

University Name, Location
Dates, Major, BFA
- Dean's List
- Minor

This solution makes good use of color and weight, but be careful about using bullets to denote tertiary information. Using too many bullets interrupts the flow of information. I almost always reduce the size of my bullets to make them less visually dominant.

Education

BFA in Major, Date
University name, Location
Minor, Dean's List

The font size remains consistent throughout, but there is still good control over the typographic hierarchy. The information is easy to scan, but students often feel a solution like this is 'boring.' Sometimes boring solutions can be effective.

Education

University Name, Location
BFA in Major | Minor
Dates | Dean's List

The designer achieves good typographic hierarchy, but has decided to use the vertical bar glyph to separate their content. In order to avoid reading the vertical bar as an 'I' extra space must be added, which can interrupt the visual flow of the text and information.

EXTENDING YOUR TYPOGRAPHIC SYSTEM

With this little résumé substudy in mind, take a minute to consider what kind of content you might include on a page in your portfolio. In many cases a portfolio piece might include information like:

Title of the piece
Page number or reference number that correlates to a table of contents
Category (e.g., Logo & Branding, Packaging, Website Design, and so forth)
A short description of the work
Any awards, recognition, or accomplishments

If you picked a typographic style for your résumé, then your challenge is to be consistent in how you use this typographic system in your portfolio and in other business-related documents. In the example below, I'm using an Education section of my résumé (left-hand side) and looking at how I can extend this typographic system into my portfolio (right-hand side) that's consistent.

Education

BFA in Graphic Design, 1996
Old Dominion University, Norfolk, Va
Cum Laude

(01)

(02)

(03)

Portfolio

The Dreamer Becomes the Designer,
A walk cycle is triggered by the act of opening the card and a series of seven images loop in a repeating sequence.

· Gold ADDY Award–Self Promotion Category, Third District American Advertising Federation Award, Blind Jury Review, Charlotte, NC.
· Gold ADDY Award–Self Promotion Category, Western Virginia American Advertising Federation Award, Blind Jury Review, Roanoke, VA.

Can You Spot the Error?

In the example above there is an inconsistency between the résumé (left) and portfolio text (right). Can you spot the error? The answer to this question is written at the bottom of the following page.

Typographic Breakdown

01. Part of the reason I chose to set my type in Minion Pro is because I wanted my dates to be set using Proportional old style numerals. Dates and date ranges can be important information, but I don't want the dates to compete with other parts of my résumé; they are a supporting element after all. If I set my dates using lining numerals the scale of the numerals appears to be set in all caps, which might create problems in my typographic hierarchy.

02. The name of the award is ADDY, which is an acronym for American Advertising Federation Award and I set text with small caps in order to prevent interrupting the flow of information and maintain the uniformity of the gray that this block of text creates. An ADDY award is something that my audience is likely to be familiar with, but it's a good idea to fully write out your acronyms if your audience might lack the information necessary to contextualize their meaning.

03. I reduced the size of the bullets and hung them slightly further to the left in order to perceptually hold the left-hand margin. I felt the bullets were necessary because I won multiple awards for this piece, but I would have eliminated them if this wasn't the case. Whenever I use bullets from here on in my portfolio or other business documents I will use them at this scale.

If you are applying for a design-related job, then you should know it's exceedingly likely you will be judged in part by the quality of your résumé. While this might seem self-evident, I see quite a few résumés that have been set using system fonts. I feel like using system fonts on your résumé is a missed opportunity because you are essentially letting your computer operating system dictate your typographic options for you. Additionally, if you're applying for a design job, touches of color are fine, but you need to be aware of how using color effects your hierarchy and flow of information.

Over the last several years I've noticed that 'information graphic-styled résumés have become increasingly popular. If you're considering adopting this type of format you need to make sure this change in format will be well-received by your audience. This

---

Answer: Look at how the name of the state is written in the résumé and how the name of the state is written in the portfolio. One is set in upper and lowercase with no punctuation and the other is written in all uppercase with punctuation. If you claim you 'have an eye for detail' in your résumé, then you better practice what you preach with regard to how you treat your content and typographic system.

consideration extends to Human Resource representatives and applicant tracking systems which may be used to filter out candidates based on keyword density algorithms. Breaking the traditional format may help you create a more active and visually appealing résumé, but you risk creating something more chaotic and less communicative. Employers still need to know you can perform certain tasks so it's imperative that you communicate that you have these specific abilities.

I often see students list a set of skills and then grade their proficiencies at these skills and I think this is a terrible structure to rate one's abilities. A much better way to show off your skills is to find clever ways to incorporate them into your work experiences. I'm not entirely sure what four out of five bullets in Adobe Illustrator means, but if you say something like "Developed logos and brand extension guidelines for organizational branding systems by utilizing my expert knowledge of Adobe Illustrator" then I feel like you've communicated your Adobe Illustrator skill set more effectively.

Keep in mind one of your goals as a designer is to create an experience others can follow easily and find an emotional attachment to. If you find yourself breaking away from established conventions just make sure you gain more than you lose—otherwise it might not be worth the effort in the long run.

ACTIONABLE ITEMS

- ❐ Create a mood board for your branding system.
- ❐ Choose, print out, and evaluate your typographic system.
- ❐ Extend your typographic system to your other business documents.

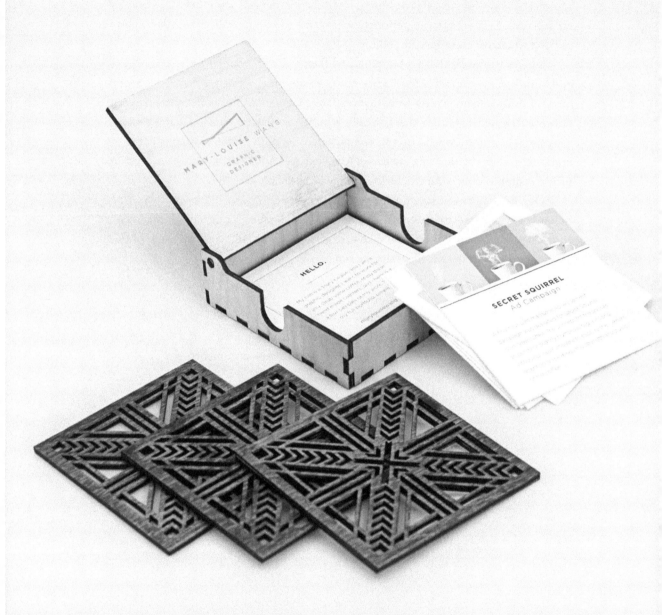

The portfolio (above) and responsive website (next page) were designed by Mary-Louise Wang.

8. Constructing Your Portfolio

There are so many options with regard to how your portfolio is constructed that it's hard to know where to begin. Construction and fabrication techniques vary greatly as do binding options, formats, and mediums. You can draw inspiration from book arts and woodworking and build your portfolio from scratch, upcycle vintage luggage you found at a swap meet, or purchase and customize your portfolio from any number of online resources. Perhaps this is what makes building a portfolio so challenging—there are so many options to choose from! No matter how you construct your portfolio or what form it takes, your portfolio needs to help you in the following ways:

- Does your portfolio (format, materials, construction, and other considerations) complement the work inside?
- Does your portfolio help you stand out (through your branding, personal narrative, or form that your portfolio takes)?
- Does your portfolio meet your needs (with regard to portability, modularity, cost, page count, how it will hold up over time, and being easy to update with new work)?

There are surprisingly few rules you have to follow, and for some people an abundance of options can make the decision seem overwhelming. However, choosing a portfolio format and construction method for your portfolio doesn't have to be such a daunting task.

It's perfectly normal to feel unsure and anxious when you are choosing a portfolio format, but typically these feelings begin to subside once you commit to a particular form. I encourage my students to take control over their anxious feelings and challenge them to transform anxiousness feelings into eager anticipation. This is an exciting time! Your body of work should be progressing nicely and you're now beginning to think

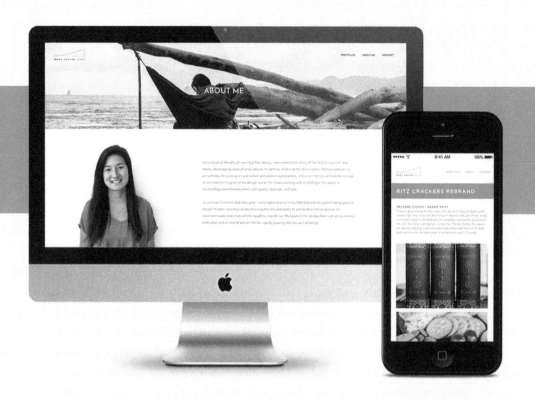

about how to design the container you'll present this work in. In order to get you through this first step (choosing your portfolio format) smoothly, here are a few pros and cons for you to consider.

BOX VERSUS BOUND PORTFOLIOS

Box Portfolios

A box portfolio is basically a shallow box or container that allows your work to lie flat. Box portfolios can be made of virtually any material from cardboard to stainless steel. Portfolio boxes usually have a hinged, fold top, or lift-off lid and come in a variety of sizes and depths. A box portfolio makes it easy to add and remove work, which can help you future-proof your portfolio. As you continue your career you'll need to replace your older work with newer work and a portfolio box makes this easy to accomplish.

Using a box portfolio format can be a smart decision if you are planning to apply for more than one type of job because it gives you the ability to switch out and reorder the work in your portfolio quite easily. A portfolio box helps reduce orientation issues, or having to rotate your portfolio 90 degrees to switch from a landscape to a portrait format. The work inside a portfolio box is often mounted on matboard and the boards are typically one-sided. Presenting work in a box portfolio can lead to an 'unboxing' component to presenting your portfolio. When done well, your presentation can be both enjoyable and participatory.

A box portfolio allows you to easily control the pace of the presentation. While all audiences might not appreciate being held captive, there can be strategic advantages to presenting your work yourself and controlling the pace. Having control over the pace can prevent someone from flipping through your work quickly and instead give yourself time to talk about your work more productively.

One consideration students sometimes fail to consider when choosing a box portfolio format is to use the space inside your portfolio box well. Your portfolio work shouldn't rattle around loosely inside the box, nor should it fit so tightly you have difficultly removing your work. Additionally, you need to take the depth of your box into consideration as well.

Your box should be filled comfortably without appearing to be too empty or overfilled. I usually try and leave around ¼" of room between the matboard and the sides of the portfolio. When the portfolio is filled with work I try and leave less than ¼" of extra space between the work and the top of the box. This means if I choose a box that is 1" deep and I use matboard that's $^1/_{16}$" thick, then I will need around 12 pieces to achieve my desired height of roughly ¾" (with a little less than ¼" of room). If I don't have 12 pieces of work

to put into my portfolio, then I'll line the bottom of my portfolio with a tightly fit piece of ¼" thick foam core or several pieces of matboard to fit 9 pieces of work perfectly.

Bound Portfolios

Bound portfolios are portfolios bound on one side, and typically function similar to that of a book. There are a wide variety of binding methods, each having its own advantages and disadvantages. Some bound portfolios come with plastic sleeves you slip work into while others may be saddle stitched, post bound, stab bound, and so forth.

How you choose to bind your portfolio can have a considerable effect on your page count and grid system. For instance, a perfect bind (similar to how most magazines are bound) requires you to have higher page count because the pages need to be glued together. The best results for perfect binding is achieved with a book that is a minimum of ¹⁄₈" thick, although most printers will tell you ¼" is preferred.

Similarly, a Japanese Stab Bound Book (shown above) will require you to experiment with the weight of the paper you use and react to the weight of the paper and binding method with your grid system. If you use a heavier paper in the book, you will notice the book becomes more difficult to open and the inside margins will need to be made larger to accommodate how a heavier paper bends when it is bound this way.

Binding methods that hold pages together by their edges (like post binding, spiral binding, and Japanese stab binding) require you to have a page count that is divisible by 2.

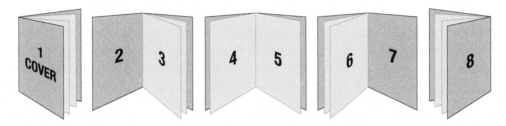

When pages are printed out in printer spreads and bound in the middle (like saddle stitching and perfect binding) you must have a page count that is divisible by 4.

Some binding methods require you to have a page count in multiples of 2, meaning each page in your portfolio has a front and back side, while other binding methods (like saddle stitching) require you to print in 'printer spreads' and dictates the number of pages in your portfolio is divisible by 4.

Why does this matter? Ideally your content will fit your portfolio like a glove and look like it was made for it. You can purchase a nice looking art portfolio for under $20 that has twenty pages with vinyl pockets to slide your work into. The problem with these portfolios is the materials often feel inexpensive and cheap and you usually cannot remove the pages you don't use.

If you have 9 pieces of work to display in your portfolio, then you'll leave almost half of your portfolio empty. I guarantee these empty pages in your portfolio will not go unnoticed. Your message to potential employers is that you are cheap and don't have a large enough body of work to fill your portfolio. Being 'cheap' and looking 'inexperienced' by not being able to fill a portfolio probably aren't messages you want to communicate.

When your body of work fits your portfolio nicely, the materials look well-considered and well-paced—you create a much more positive experience for your audience. People react positively when things are clear and understandable. Something so simple as a page count or binding format shouldn't raise questions or draw your audience's attention away from what you are trying to communicate or show through your body of work. It's perfectly fine to show you can work with various formats, construction methods, and materials, but these decisions should appear as intentional decisions rather than default decisions that were dictated to you.

Additionally, it can be more difficult to switch work in and out of some bound portfolio formats. Making changes to a saddle stitched, perfect bound, or Japanese stab bound documents might require you to reprint and rebind your entire document if you spot an error or want to make changes to your document. However, bound portfolios can usually be produced more cheaply in higher quantities than most box portfolios. This is a consideration you might want to entertain if you think it might be advantageous to leave your portfolio behind after an interview, plan on shipping your portfolio to a potential employer, or want to share a copy of your portfolio with your family and friends.

When done well, bound portfolios are beautiful! Bound portfolios can be smaller and lighter than box portfolios. In some cases, your body of work can be laid out and printed using software like Adobe InDesign, which also gives you the advantage of being able to quickly and easily create an interactive PDF version of your portfolio.

Undoubtedly, part of the responsibilities for the position you're applying for requires you to make good decisions. You can choose any binding method for your portfolio that you want, so make a good decision. Choose a binding method that complements your body of work and needs, rather than making a decision you'll be forced to fight against later. Any blank pages that appear in your portfolio should appear intentional and strategic rather than being perceived as having to stretch your content to fit a particular page count or format.

SHOULD YOU PURCHASE OR BUILD YOUR PORTFOLIO?

Whatever style of portfolio you decide to go (box or bound) with it's worth your time to think about the pros and cons of how your portfolio will function. You don't want to outgrow your portfolio too quickly and have to recreate it again in a year to two. You'll want your portfolio to hold up to the physical aspects of traveling with it and using it to apply to jobs, so considerations like size, weight, and portability should also factor into your decision.

The portfolio shown above was built from a $2.00 wooden cigar box. The labels and paint were stripped, the box was sanded and repainted in a glossy black finish, and the interior was recovered in fabric.

If you plan on purchasing a portfolio, try to see if you can find a vendor who has one in stock or ask around to see if anyone in your network has one you can look at in person. If this isn't possible, then make sure to do your research and look at online comments, feedback, and reviews from people who have purchased the portfolio. Make sure you identify what comes with the portfolio or if you'll have to purchase other components separately. Items like sheet protectors, screw posts, adhesive strips, and other items may be sold separately or sometimes purchased from other vendors more inexpensively.

You will need to customize your portfolio, so don't forget to add in those expenses also. Many companies offer laser cutting, embossing, screen printing, UV coatings, and other options to help you customize your portfolio, but don't be afraid to experiment and look for nontraditional alternatives to customize your portfolio. Stickers, tip-ins, and other techniques can be equally effective and often cheaper ways to customize your portfolio. However, it's important to understand that no matter which technique(s) you use your craftsmanship needs to be impeccable. Purchase enough supplies to test out an unfamiliar process or material(s) before applying it to your portfolio. Make sure you're in good control over your techniques and mediums so you don't unintentionally send the wrong message to your audience.

Before you purchase a portfolio or begin constructing your portfolio take a moment to think about the orientation of your portfolio. If you're considering a bound portfolio, then the orientation of your portfolio can have a considerable impact on how your work is displayed. There are 3 orientations you can choose to present your work—landscape, portrait, or square. While a capable designer could create a portfolio in any of these orientations the best format to choose is the format that mirrors that of your body of work and the conditions in which your portfolio will be viewed.

Every semester I see a few students make decisions with regard to the orientation of their portfolio, struggle, and then change the orientation of their portfolio about halfway through the semester, causing them to waste lots of time and energy. If I can offer you some sage advice it would be this—consider the natural orientation of your work and work with that particular format rather than working against it. It's often difficult to visualize what a portfolio is going to look like when you first begin constructing it. Each design decision you make either reinforces one of your previous design decision or introduces a new variable for consideration. Generally speaking, graphic designers often start building a system by looking at the content and seeing how the various pieces might fit together in an orderly way.

Inside your portfolio you will need to show large pictures of your work as well as detail shots of areas of interest. If you choose a portfolio orientation that doesn't work with your content, then you won't be able to include as many large images of your work and you'll be forced to deal with areas of unintended/unplanned white space.

It's okay if you have a few vertical pieces in a landscape portfolio (and vice versa), but designing your portfolio becomes a whole lot easier when you choose an orientation that works with your content. I have to admit I was tempted to work in square format at first myself, but after playing with my grid system and content for a couple of hours I had to step back and assess whether my content was fighting this orientation.

When I stepped back and looked at the work more objectively I also felt that a landscape format would work well for my website and PDF portfolio since most monitors and computer screens are in a landscape format. I knew that my audience would look at my work on a computer monitor rather than a mobile device, so this helped further reinforce this design decision. I also knew that it would likely create less work for me to photograph and mock-up my work in one orientation, rather than mocking everything up in both a horizontal and vertical format.

While I was honestly a little resistant to creating a landscape portfolio at first, I'm exceedingly happy with my results in the end. When I realized I was forcing my content to fit a format for no particular reason I made a difficult decision to change my format. In

Look through your body of work to see if there is a natural orientation that you can take advantage of in your portfolio. If you tend to shoot in a landscape orientation, you might want to duplicate this format in your portfolio.

the end it was the best design decision I could have made to showcase my work—which is really the point of a portfolio after all, right? Sometimes it's easy to forget why you're making these design decisions in the heat of the moment. If you find yourself really banging your head against the wall struggling it might be a good idea to take a break and look at your work with fresh eyes, get a critique from someone you trust, or look at precedence for how others have solved similar problems in the past.

TIPS FOR USING TYPOGRAPHY WELL
Choosing Your Typefaces

When I choose the typefaces I'm going to use in a project I'm looking for a few specific things. I try to limit myself to 1 or 2 typefaces for a project and I try to pick typefaces that have a diverse font family. A diverse typeface may have light, book, regular, semibold, bold, and black variations in weight, proportion, and posture. A typeface this robust can be used to create typographic hierarchy more easily than a typeface which only has regular and bold options available.

When I use two typefaces in a project I try to understand how the typefaces are both different and similar to each other. For example, I may want my two typefaces to contrast each other so I can use one for headings and headlines and the other for body copy and other content. Perhaps the contrast I'm looking for is achieved by the contrast of visual weights of the two typefaces, or perhaps it is a combination of using a serif and a sans-serif typeface. There are many typographic variables you can use to create contrast, so some basic understanding of typographic and design principles may prove useful.

While establishing typographic contrast is important, I've learned that working with typefaces that share a similar x-height can be beneficial—particularly when working on a baseline grid. So I will pick a contrasting typeface with similar x-height (or the distance from the baseline to the meanline) in order to establish a sense of typographic unity, or the feeling that all of the typographic elements are working together as a whole.

As mentioned in Chapter 7, there are a variety of online resources available to you if you don't feel comfortable choosing good typographic pairings; however, one of the most important steps you can take is to objectively look at your work in the environment it is intended to be viewed in. Type that was created for on-screen environments may function poorly in print environments and vice versa. If you are creating a print and digital version of your portfolio, then you will want to choose typeface(s) which holds up well in both of these environments. The only way to know for sure if your type will hold up is to test it on screen and to make hard copy samples.

Consistency Throughout

It's likely you will need to use the same typeface(s) for your portfolio, résumé, and website because these typefaces will become part of your branding system—along with other visual elements. Using your type consistently is important because it can assist you in establishing a rhythm and cohesive quality to your portfolio and professional documents. When you establish a 'rule' in one of your professional documents you should follow that same protocol in all of your documents for consistency.

Typographic consistency isn't just limited to typefaces and rules, but to how you use space within your documents as well. The spacing within and between typographic elements needs to be used consistently also. Establishing a baseline grid and using Character, Object, and Paragraph Styles within InDesign can help you compose your work quickly and maintain typographic consistency in your printed and digital documents.

Objects and Paragraph Styles mirror how Cascading Style Sheets (CSS) can be used to establish a stylistic rules that can be applied to tags in HTML documents. You set up a rule and then apply your rule to the selected content. There are a number of good online resources you can access to learn about Character, Object, and Paragraph Styles which include tutorials from Adobe.com. One of the lesser known aspects of Character, Object, and Paragraph Styles is that they can be easily exported from one document and imported into another. This means that you can quickly establish typographic consistency between your documents with a minimum amount of effort. If you go on a job interview and state, "One of my strengths is that I pay attention to details" and then fail to pay attention to the details of your typographic decision-making, then you might get called out on it.

Choosing the Right Glyphs

Designers are often held to a higher standard with their typographic decisions than many other disciplines, but everyone can benefit from brief typographic refresher. Often computer operating systems and software make incorrect typographic decisions for us and it's important to know when an error has occurred and fix it. Here is a short list of common typographic errors and also glyphs you should look for when choosing your typefaces to use. Many of the following glyphs are easy to access in InDesign by simply going to Type > Glyphs and typing the name of what you are looking for into the search bar. Double click the glyph to insert it into your text box.

Glyph	When to use it
'	Use straight single quotations marks to indicate feet (measurement).
"	Use straight double quotations marks to indicate inches (measurement).
" "	Use double left- and double right-quotation marks for quotations.
' '	Use single left- and single right-quotation marks for quotations within another quotation (e.g., "That is a 'magic' hat.")
-	Use a hyphen between compound adjectives (e.g., Long-term plan).
—	Use an en-dash to connect values in a range (e.g., 2013–17)
——	Use an em-dash as a stand-in for a comma or parenthesis to separate out phrases—or even just a word—in a sentence.
¼	Use properly set fractions. There's a big difference between ¼ cup of sugar and 1/4 cup. Proper fractions are more compatible with text that has been set in upper and lowercase.
×	Use the proper multiplication glyph (e.g., 1024×768) instead of using a lowercase x.
…	Use the ellipses glyph instead of three periods in a row.

TITLE OF THE PIECE

This is a description of the piece. Descriptions are usually a couple of sentences to a few short paragraph long. You usually describe the project, your goals, any unique constraints you accepted, and your project outcome(s).

TIPS FOR DEVELOPING A GRID SYSTEM

Often a designer will develop a grid system to help them make decisions more quickly and consistently. He or she pays special attention to the shortest and longest content (the outliers) knowing if he or she can handle this content well, then the more common pieces of content are likely to take care of themselves. If the designer were to create his or her system by focusing on the more common pieces of content first, then the outliers risk standing out as being different—weakening the overall strength of the system.

When I design a grid system I take both my content and typography into consideration. I pay attention to the dimensions of my content as well as how my typography looks under optimal conditions. I begin by setting fake headlines and body copy, then I choose my typeface(s) and sizes. I test to see how the content looks and continue to make small changes to my text (typeface, point size, tracking, leading, and so forth) until I'm satisfied. Since this grid system will be for my portfolio, I know I'll need to test to see how the typeface functions in both print and digital environments.

Once I'm satisfied with how my type has been set, I want to create a grid system that is built off of the dimensions of my type. For example, I've chosen Open Sans Condensed Bold, 13 point text for my headlines because it is free to use (fonts.google.com), it's available as a web font—meaning I can use this same font for my online and print portfolio, and I like how it looks. For my body copy I'm going to use Open Sans Regular, 8.75 point text and reduce the size of this type to help establish more contrast between the headlines and my body copy to create a greater sense of typographic hierarchy.

Set Up Your Baseline Grid

I've decided that my print portfolio is going to be printed on 11"×17" paper in a landscape format since most of the content for my portfolio is in a landscape format already. This orientation also works nicely in online environments. The next step is to set up a baseline grid because I want all of the elements (images, graphics, and so forth) on the page to complement the vertical spacing of my type.

Notice how the top of the image (shown as a black box) aligns with the capline of the title to the right.

I know from experience sometimes text and images don't visually line up when they are aligned to a baseline grid, so instead of creating a baseline grid that is spaced out every 10 pixels, I'm going to divide this dimension by half and use a 5-point baseline grid instead. This means my text will line up on every other baseline grid, but it also gives me an opportunity to align the top of my images to the capline of my titles and body copy. While I initially set my leading manually, once my baseline grid has been determined I'll snap my text to my baseline grid instead. These alignments can help create a sense of harmony and provide both structure and flexibility to the designer.

Set Your Margins and Rows

I need to determine what my top-, bottom-, left-, and right-hand margins will be. I re-searched how I'm going to construct my portfolio and bind my pages, and I've decided to purchase a black (onyx) Pina Zangaro portfolio with a screw post bind and mount clear plastic hinge strips to the back of my portfolio pages. The hinge strips are self-adhesive strips and are placed on the back of the 11"×17" page, which is nice because it allows me to use the entire page to showcase my design solutions. Because the hinge strips adhere to the back of my work, I don't need to leave extra room in my inside margin to account for how my portfolio is bound. I've also decided because the hinge strips adhere on the back of the page, that I'm going to leave the back of my portfolio pages blank. If you decide to bind your work in a different way, you may need to leave extra room in your inside margin to account for your particular binding method.

I know I want my page to be divided into 12 horizontal rows with a roughly ½" mar-gin on the top, bottom, left, and right, so the total number of lines that I can fit vertically on the page will need to be divisible by 12. Through a little trial and error, I found I can fit 72 lines of 8.75/10 point type on the page, leaving me a little over ½" margins (0.5694" to be exact). Seventy two lines of type can be divided by 12 rows easily, which avoids leaving any awkward vertical space left over.

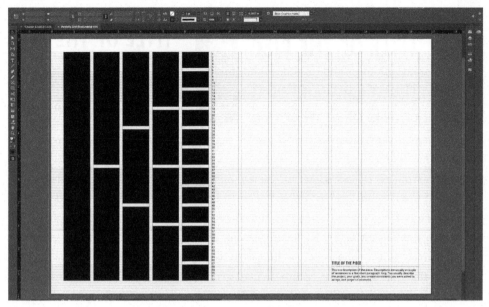

Dividing your composition up into 12 rows and columns allows you to create visual compositions with a number of mathematical options. You can download this grid system by going to bhannam.com/grid.zip and the font Open Sans can be downloaded at fonts.google.com

Create Columns

I'm going to need my grid system to appear on every page in my document, so I'll double click on my Master Page and make my top-, bottom-, left-, and right-hand margins 0.5694" and create 12 vertical columns by going to Layout > Margins and Columns and increasing the number of columns to 12. While I have this window open, I will also make my gutters 10 points wide (or 1 em-dash) in order to reuse the same dimension I used for my leading, but this time vertically.

Use Your Grid

I like having 10 points of horizontal and vertical space between each of the modules in my grid system. This 10 point space prevents content from bumping into other content and makes the grid system quite flexible to use. I also like that my grid system was developed through observing my typography in its ideal state first and the rest of the grid system was developed by reusing these dimensions. Together, all of these nuances and details support each other to create a sense of unity within the system.

When you have a solid foundation in place, you can riff and build off of it in some fun and often unexpected ways. Grids can be used to establish a meter, rhythm, organization, hierarchy, and proportion. When used well they can help make your work look

THERE ARE NO PORTFOLIO CONSTRAINTS

(OTHER THAN THOSE YOU CHOOSE TO ACCEPT)

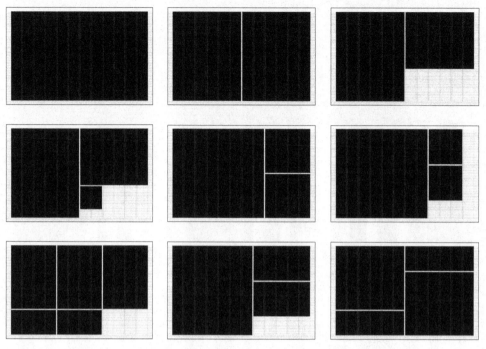

Even though every spread is different, your grid system is the unifying element that connects them all.

intentional and focused as well as helping create opportunities where you can break free from the grid system to create emphasis. Grid systems can also encourage you use white space more effectively within your compositions.

One thing is clear, understanding the limits of a grid system can only really come from experience, so play around with your grid system and experiment! I'm always surprised when I see students painstakingly create a grid system and then abandon it three pages into their portfolio. If you've put together a good grid system, then it should speed up the design process. You should find your grid system makes laying out placeholder text and boxes easier, and helps you be more productive when preparing to photograph your work by helping 1) identify how many shots of your work you'll need and 2) determine the orientation and proportions of photographs.

Typically, this is the time where my students begin to develop a sense of what their portfolio will look like when it's finished. There are still lots of decisions left to make, but you can probably begin to extrapolate information to catch a glimpse of how your portfolio might look in the end. If you don't like the direction your portfolio is going for any reason, then this is a good time to adjust your course. It's perfectly natural to feel anxious, nervous, or to second guess yourself, but resist the urge to throw out your work

FRANK OCEAN CONCERT POSTER
This is a concert poster for R&B singer/songwriter Frank Ocean's headlining performance at Panorama Music Festival. The fragmentation of the type and the leaves speak to the nature of a "panorama", while communicating the musician's aesthetic and present style. The poster could be used as print or digital flyers prior to the concert, or could be sold at the artist's merchandise table during the festival.

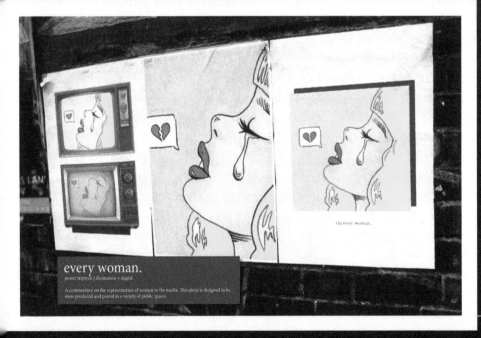

Top: A page from Rachel Hayes' portfolio (using the tabloid size grid system mentioned on the previous pages). Bottom: A page from Erin Mena's portfolio (using the same grid system).

> *"In many cases the best way to photograph your work is to stage it in the environment for which it was created."*

and start over again. As you begin to catch your first glimpses of your portfolio it's perfectly natural to panic, but throwing all your work out and starting over again isn't going to remedy these feelings. Making changes to your initial direction are a perfectly natural part of the design process, but it's very likely that starting over from scratch is simply a bad decision. Don't let fear creep into your thoughts and make you start second guessing yourself. You've spent all this time developing a plan—now execute it impeccably.

TIPS FOR TAKING GOOD PHOTOGRAPHS

In many cases the best way to photograph your work is to stage it in the environment for which it was created. These environments provide the audience with subtle clues about the appropriateness of your solution. In my opinion, posters always look better when photographed hung up on a wall rather than floating in the ether of space. A lowly business card design can look amazing when photographed being pulled out of a business card holder and handed out to an implied viewer. Simply put, all kinds of information can be embedded in how you photograph your work and you can use photography to amplify how your work is perceived.

That said, here are some relatively easy tips you can use to get amazing photographs of your work. These tips have one thing in common—they are all inexpensive and easy to implement. No expensive tools or equipment is necessary to pull off these simple photography tips and tricks.

Work in High Resolution

Most of the newer digital cameras have plenty of resolution for beginning photographers, which means resolution isn't as important as it used to be. Since there's no 'standard' number for a high-resolution photograph determining what's considered high resolution can be different from person to person. If your camera allows you to choose a resolution, then shoot in the highest resolution available. It's easy enough to scale an image down in Photoshop, but it's harder to make an image look good when scaling it up. By working and editing your photographs in the highest resolution possible and scaling them as your final step, you can make sure your photographs are always free from pixilation, compression, and other digital artifacts.

Notice how the energy of these two photographs changes as adjustments to lighting and the angle of attack are made? The image on the left is gray and lacks energy, while the image on the right is well lit and moves the viewers' eyes through the composition in a more controlled way.

Take Lots (And I Mean Lots) of Photographs

Taking photographs of your work isn't hard, but it can be time consuming and you will save yourself time and energy by getting the shot you need the first time. When you photograph a piece take lots of shots and make adjustments to your angle of attack, framing, orientation, focus, lighting, shutter speed, f-stop, ISO, distance to the subject, layout, and other variables. You never know when you'll need images of your work so by taking lots of pictures when you have the chance you're 1) giving yourself options to choose from, 2) preventing having to duplicate a photography session in the future, and 3) giving yourself ample space around the objects you are photographing to give you additional design options later.

Even though you'll end up cropping many of your photographs tightly in your portfolio, a little extra padding around your work makes the design phase a little easier down the line. On several occasions I've run into a problem where I need to add text to my image (e.g., for a hero on a website), but I was so focused on cropping my images tight during my photography session that I never even thought of taking a few shots where I was zoomed out of my work. I spent an entire Saturday afternoon setting up my work (again) just to get an image with a little extra padding around it.

When you take the time to set up and stage your images, make sure to take establishing, full-view, and detail shots of your work. Establishing shots are images that are designed to introduce the audience to a new scene (or piece) and introduce all of the parts of a project. A full-view shot is an image that uses the full height or width of the frame to show the most important element, and a detail shot takes the audience closer to the work to reveal a particular element or design decision. All three of these shots serve a particular purpose and should be used to orient your audience, focus their attention, or draw their attention to a particular area.

Your audience is looking at your portfolio because they want to see examples of your best work, so take photographs that take them to the action! When you layout your portfolio, remove the extra padding around your photographs and crop your images tightly. Is your solution a little unconventional and difficult to explain? Take an establishing shot to help define the context for your solution. Is there a component of the project that needs to stand out or be displayed prominently? If so, photograph it as a full shot—using the full width or height of the image to create a strong sense of page hierarchy. Do you have a place in your design where you dealt with a difficult constraint or an area where you feel like you were extra creative? Take detail shots of this area by zooming in.

A common mistake I see young designers make with their photography is creating a layout with an establishing shot and a detail shot, but they don't actually zoom into their work in the detail shot. The distance to the subject doesn't change significantly and the detail shot comes across as being repetitive rather than highlighting or drawing your audience's attention to one of your design decisions. What's the point of that? Remember, don't rush the process of photographing your work. Give yourself time to experiment and take lots of photographs with little variations and adjustments.

Punch Up Your Images

I've touched up absolutely every photo in my portfolio and you should consider doing so too. Here are a few easy steps you can take in Adobe Photoshop to help enhance your portfolio images.

- **Cropping:** One of the easiest ways to improve your images is to crop them well. Crop out distracting or unnecessary information to keep your viewers' attention focused on your work. Your audience wants to see your solution, so crop it tightly enough to maximize the space you have allocated for the image in your layout. It's such an easy oversight to make, but it's something I've seen numerous students forget to do.

- **Color correction:** There are some great tutorials you can find online about strategies for color correcting your images. Unfortunately, there isn't a one-size-fits-all solution for color correcting photographs in various lighting conditions. You'll probably want to make the colors and lighting of your work as realistically as possible in order to highlight your design decisions rather than your photography skills.

- **Sharpening your images:** Here's an easy tip to accentuate the details in your photographs, use a high pass filter to sharpen your images. Simply open your image up in

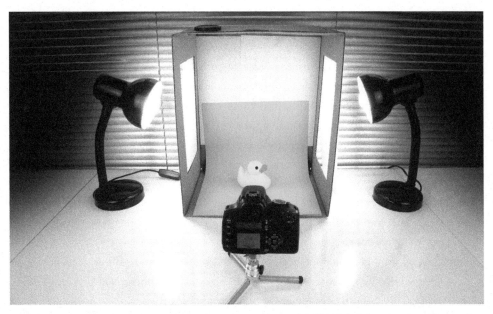

You don't need high-end equipment to get good shots of your work. This light box was created from a cardboard box, sheer fabric, poster board, and two desk lamps. There are numerous video tutorials online with step-by-step instructions you can follow to make a light box of your own.

Photoshop and perform all of your other edits first (cropping, color correction, and so forth). When you're finished editing your image, go to Layer > Duplicate, which will duplicate your image and place it on another layer. Select the top layer by clicking on it once and go to Filter > Other > High Pass and enter a value (typically a value between 5–10 pixels works well). Your image will probably turn an ugly gray, but don't worry we aren't finished yet. Go back to your Layers palette and choose 'Overlay' from the drop down menu where you specify your blend mode (typically set to 'normal'). Your image should now appear much sharper, particularly with regard to your typography and edge contours. You can dial in the level of sharpness in your image by changing the opacity of your top layer.

- **Batch Editing:** If you find yourself repeating a particular step repeatedly in Photoshop you might want to look into creating an action in the Actions window. Actions are simply a series of steps that can be recorded and then reapplied at any time, and allows you to recreate an end result quickly without having to go through each individual step every time. This is a shortcut that can save you time by automating steps that you use frequently. This process can also be used as a means of eliminating user errors because your values are recorded and can be used consistently when working with a large number of images.

Staging Your Shots

You don't need a lot of equipment to photograph your work: a camera, a light source, and perhaps a tripod is all you really need. I prefer shooting my work with a DSLR because it allows me to change my camera lenses and can shoot in a RAW file format. Appropriate lighting is essential, and studio lighting can help you keep your light sources and levels consistent although you can photograph your work in natural lighting. If you don't have access to a studio, try and pick an environment that has lots of natural, even-lit light.

I like to try to photograph my work in the type of environment for which it was created and I try to incorporate little visual context clues in my photographs to help provide my audience with some insights or backstory about my solution. As such, I find myself raiding local fabric and craft stores for fabric, paper, candles, ribbons, fruit, candy, or other supplies to incorporate into my images.

When I set up a shot I have to decide how active I want my composition to be. For some solutions I need an active and engaging image, so I'll try and create an asymmetrical composition with depth cues (layering, shadows, blurring, changes in scale, and so forth). I may photograph my work with a steep angle of attack in order to create a sense of energy within the photograph. Other times I want my audience to take in my work and want my background to appear more calm and neutral. In these cases I might choose a symmetrical composition and create a cloth or paper backdrop to remove distracting elements from my photograph. I may photograph my work from the front and lower my angle of attack. The point is, you can stage your shot and alter how you photograph your work to help you tell your story and capture an image of your work in a flattering way.

Personally, I feel a portfolio should generally contain a sense of energy and excitement, so I usually try to stage and photograph my work to convey this feeling to my audience. Since I'm being hired to do something I want my portfolio to covey a certain energy level and enthusiasm—as if I approached every day of work with a high energy level. Yes, there are projects where it's less appropriate to portray them this way, but when I have the opportunity to photograph my work in an environment and with a certain energy level I typically fall back to this line of thinking.

Purchasing items to stage your portfolio can be expensive! Whenever possible I try to purchase high-quality items to use in my photographs (and I try to keep the tags on and the receipt handy so I can return the items for a refund later). I remember once in college I was staging a photo shoot for a wine label I created and I purchased plastic grapes to use to stage my work. Once my film was developed I realized how my decision to use plastic grapes cheapened the quality of my design solution. I vowed never to make the same mistake again!

Setting Up Your Lighting

Let's face it, lighting is arguably the biggest factor in taking a good photograph. You don't need expensive equipment to get a good shot, but you do need to understand the role in which lighting plays.

You might not be familiar with the lighting terminology, so here is a quick overview of some common terms along with a tried-and-true method of setting up your lighting sources.

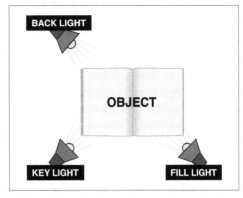

This illustrates how three-point lighting is often set up by using a key light, fill light, and a back light.

Lighting Terminology

Key Light: A key light is the first and usually most important light that a photographer uses in a lighting setup. The purpose of a key light is to highlight the form and dimension of the work. Usually your key light will be the strongest light you'll use, but that doesn't mean you should crank up your key light to full power by default—it means your key light will probably be your dominant light source.

Fill Light: A fill light is often used to soften the shadows made by the key light in order to make them seem lighter and less dramatic. This light is usually set to be approximately half as intense as the key light to keep from canceling out the effects of the key light out. In many cases your fill light will be placed lower than your key light because it serves as a secondary light source with a less dominant role.

Back Light: A back light's job is to illuminate the subject/object from the back and to help define the edges of the subject/object. A back light shouldn't be confused with a 'background light,' which lights background elements. Backlighting helps separate the subject from the background.

Do It Yourself Three-Point Lighting

Three-Point Lighting is a method of lighting that is commonly used in still theatre, video, and still photography. You can create a three-point lighting system from inexpensive desk lamps or light sources you already own, but there are a few factors to consider which will make photographing your work much easier.

- **Use the same type of light bulbs:** This seems like a silly tip, but not all light bulbs are created equally. Incandescent, LED, CFL, halogen, and other types of light bulbs have different wattages, color temperatures, and so forth. If you set up your lighting using different types of light bulbs, then you're going to have a difficult time getting your camera's white balance feature to work properly. Choose a light bulb with a sufficient amount of lumens (lumens measure the amount of light produced, watts measure the amount of energy required) and check the color temperature of the light bulbs. The color temperature of a light bulb is measured in Kelvin and a light with a low Kelvin rating (3,500K or less) is referred to as a warm light and has a soft, yellow-orange glow. A light with a high Kelvin rating (6,000K or more) is referred to as being cool and has a bluish white quality. Either color bulb can work well, but it's best not to mix the color of your bulbs when setting up your lighting. If you are photographing your work in a room where daylight will also be entering, then try and use a light bulb that is 'daylight' balanced and has a color temperature of around 5,000K. This will help ensure that all of your lighting is the same color temperature and gives you the best results.

- **Use Dimmable Lights:** While it's not impossible to control your light levels using a piece of sheer cloth or other object, dimmable lights can make controlling the brightness of your light sources far easier. Your key light will be your primary light source, but your fill light is usually around half as bright.

- **Use a Tripod:** In order to get the best photographs you'll need to use a tripod. Being able to hold your camera steady—especially when using a slow shutter speed or low f-stop will help your images look nice and sharp. In addition, there have been many occasions where I'm photographing a piece of work (like a menu) where I only have one copy. If I put my camera on a tripod I can take a picture and then reposition the menu and take a second image. Because the camera hasn't moved, it's extremely easy to composite the two images together in Photoshop in order to create a composition where you can see the cover of the menu and an interior spread. This would be far more difficult to accomplish if the camera had moved.

- **Use Reflectors:** Reflectors can be made from illustration board, silver wrapping paper, or aluminum foil and a couple of binder clips to help hold them in place. You can use reflectors to bounce and reflect light in order to take one light source and create a fill light, backlight, or kicker.

- **Think About Your Lens and Aperture:** When shooting a product shot, you might want to avoid using a wide angle lens. These lenses tend to distort the shape of the object. If you want a shot where all of your object is in focus, then you might also want to avoid using a wide aperture like f2.8 or f4.5 because a wide aperture will narrow your depth of field and leave part of your product out of focus. A small aperture like f8 or f11 will give you a wider depth of field and keep your product in focus.

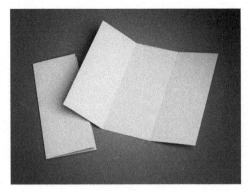

Mock-ups, like stock photography, have to be used with care. While they allow you to work quickly, mock-ups can be overused easily.

USE MOCK-UPS SPARINGLY

Using mock-ups to display your work is a double-edged sword. Mock-ups are digital files that can be downloaded or purchased online and used to display your work quickly and easily. Mock-ups allow you to use software like Adobe Photoshop, Illustrator, or InDesign to create a computer mock-up your work instead of having to create physical copies of your work and photograph it.

Mock-ups can sometimes help you achieve a printing effect or technique like an embossed logo or reflective UV varnish which can sometimes be helpful to show you've considered how your work will be produced in their final form.

While mock-ups can speed up your workflow, they sometimes come at a cost—it's easy to lose your visual voice when you depend on others to make design decisions for you. For example, you can see how the mock-up above has been personalized, but I can't really control all of the design elements in the mock-up. Some decisions like the angle of attack, lighting, and composition have been predetermined. Additionally, I'm unable to tell how many other designers used this mock-up in their portfolio, so rather than having my work stand out, I may unintentionally make my work blend in.

I've been teaching graphic design for over 15 years and over the years I've encountered numerous mock-ups. These days I've become exceedingly good at not only spotting when mock-ups have been used, but I can now also identify where they were purchased or downloaded.

Some audiences react negatively to mock-ups, while others accept them as part of a larger strategy. Personally, I feel that as long as mock-ups play a supporting role in a designer's portfolio rather than the primary role, then I'm okay with using them to supplement a portfolio. My preference would be to have the designer take their own images of

Are you sure your mock-up is sending the right message? There's a lot of distractions in the backgrounds of these images that are going to contextualize your work.

their work, but I understand that this isn't always feasible. Sometimes you simply don't have access to a vacuum press or have the ability to print on cardboard and a mock-up might provide you with some good options. Other times, you should simply print out your poster, hang it up, and photograph it yourself.

It's important to realize that not all mock-ups are created equally. Take a look at the mock-up shown above and notice how much contextual and potentially distracting information has been included in these photographs.

When you're looking for a mock-up, you have to look at your images semiotically. Visual semiotics is an analysis of the way visual images communicate a message. The top left image of the man by the pool can be interpreted as having a casual feel (the man has his shoes off and is sitting by the pool). This image has a busy background and it looks as if the photographer has tried to neutralize the busy background by using a lens with a shallow depth of field (blurring the background) with so-so success. The image on the right has a man holding a poster. He appears as if a houseplant is attacking him and the photographer's flash is casting a harsh shadow on the wall behind him.

In both of these photographs the background elements appear to be quite active, but stop to consider how much real estate has been devoted to showing off the work on the laptop screen and poster. Less than 25% of the entire image showcases the work and both of these mock-ups would function poorly if used as an establishing shot in your portfolio. While you might be able to crop these images and use them as a full shot, they still require your attention and probably aren't ready to be dropped into your portfolio in their current condition. If I was looking for a mock-up and saw these images, I probably wouldn't choose to work with either of them.

Before you purchase a mock-up it's important to look at the image rights and see what rights you have. Some websites will sell you an inexpensive mock-up, but only

TRY TO USE MOCK-UPS SPARINGLY

provide you with limited rights. For example, if you purchased a mock-up with a regular license on a popular website the mock-up will cost you $4.00 and come with a regular license. A regular license allows you to use the mock-up in one end product—as long as that end product isn't sold. *Translation: A $4.00 mock-up is fine to use in your portfolio.* But let's pretend for a moment that I contacted you and invited you to publish your work in this book (which will be sold), then the regular license you purchased for $4.00 is no longer sufficient. You'd be forced to repurchase the mock-up—this time with an extended license—which costs $55.00.

Sometimes it takes some effort to read through and understand Image Licensing distinctions, so if you're ever in doubt it's probably best to contact the company directly. Most of the time a 'regular' license is sufficient, but each vendor sets their own policies for image usage and it's important to look before you leap.

WRITING TITLES AND DESCRIPTIONS OF YOUR WORK

It's common for hiring managers and Creative Directors to meet your portfolio before they meet you, and your titles and descriptions can help to better understand and contextualize your work. There's a saying that goes, "You only get one chance to make a first impression," and it means people often make determinations quickly—it's critical to make a good first impression. Each piece in your portfolio needs to have a title and a short description. On the surface it sounds easy, but descriptions of your work shouldn't be more than a paragraph or two in length. As such you will have to edit what you say about yourself, your design process, and your work. For many, this is where the challenge in writing descriptions of your work begins.

Titling Your Work

Your title of your pieces should be short and memorable. Portfolios are generally viewed quickly, so use your titles as a way of providing insight into the piece, your design process, or to help you tell your story.

A good title is memorable and catchy. Try to be original, but don't err on the side of being cheesy. It's best to avoid using acronyms unless you feel certain your audience will recognize the reference. When choosing a title, avoid being redundant. If the piece is a poster you created for a local library, then don't title the piece 'Library Poster.' Instead, approach your title as an additional element to your solution that delivers insight.

I try to keep the length of my titles at a fairly uniform length because I know the titles will inevitably be used as a navigation element or viewed in a Table of Contents at some point. I don't want the length of my titles to be perceived as a hierarchical element, suggesting that a piece is somehow less important because it's shorter. In addition, you can create opportunities to subtly keyword stuff your portfolio. Look for clues in a job description about which keywords to incorporate into your titles.

Writing Descriptions of Your Work

When writing about a piece, refrain from writing a long introduction. Instead, consider using the PAR formula to describe your work. PAR is an acronym for Problem + Action = Result, and it can be a useful formula to help frame the description of your work.

- **Problem:** Describe how and/or why the project was initiated. Identify any unique constraints or challenges you faced. What was the challenge(s) or primary objective(s)? Who was the intended audience? If appropriate, describe the client's background. As a designer you're not just hired for style, but also the clarity in which you interpret a creative brief. This can be important information to a hiring manager and an aspect that is easy to overlook in a project description.
- **Action:** Describe what steps you took to solve the problem. If applicable, describe your design process, insights and discoveries, techniques, methods, technologies, or steps you took to meet the client's objective(s).
- **Result:** Describe how your solution was received by the client, the intended audience, and/or the design community. Did your solution win any awards? Did it exceed your client's expectations? Was the primary objective met? Were you able to heighten awareness or successfully target a particular audience? Were there any measurable results? Do you have any client testimonials?

Final Steps to Take

It goes without saying that spelling and grammar are of the utmost importance, but it's equally important to control the flow of ideas and write lucid, relevant descriptions. Make sure to highlight collaborations and, if working in a group or team environment, the role you played. It's important to give credit where credit is due so make sure to mention your university, agency, professors, peers, teammates, and collaborators when it is appropriate to do so.

With these questions and strategies in mind you can probably see why writing a short description of your work can be challenging. You'll need to prioritize your information and edit out much of your tertiary and supporting information in order to keep your audience's attention from waning. Have someone not familiar with your work read through your descriptions and give you feedback about how articulate and easily understood your descriptions are.

MAKING YOUR WORK THE STAR OF THE SHOW

Now that you have a portfolio format, typography, photographs, titles and descriptions, a grid system, and branding elements there's only one thing left to do—put it all together. Just make sure your work is the star of the show. Your work is more important that any of the other elements in your portfolio, so highlight your work. Every element of your portfolio should help support, contextualize, and show off your hard work.

Be careful that the other elements in your portfolio enhance your work rather than compete with it. If you discover your branding system is too strong (visually) when constructing your portfolio, then take steps to tone it down. The success of your portfolio hinges upon the strength of your work and displaying it well.

ANYTHING GOES. BE SURPRISING. CREATE AN EXPERIENCE.

There's no 'right way' to build a portfolio because there are an infinite number of materials, techniques, strategies, and audiences. A killer portfolio is one that aligns with your unique constraints, body of work, and audience.

Make sure you leave time for receiving feedback, experimenting with new materials and techniques, and craftsmanship. My students almost always underestimate the amount of time it takes to write their descriptions and print out their portfolio work. Make sure you leave yourself enough time to address problems when something doesn't work out the way you planned—which is sure to happen.

If you identified your audience and their needs, developed a good strategy, edited and curated your work, and branded yourself well, then the act of going through your portfolio will create a unique and memorable experience. Each page in your portfolio should look unique, but part of a larger system. Your work will be prominently displayed, with a clear hierarchical order on the page, with strategic descriptions and unique branding elements. Congratulations, you're well on your way to creating a killer portfolio that's unique to you.

ACTIONABLE ITEMS

- ☐ Pick a portfolio orientation based off of your body of work.
- ☐ Develop a grid system based off of your typographic decisions and binding methods.
- ☐ Photograph your work, capturing establishing and detail shots as you go.
- ☐ Write clear and succinct titles and descriptions for your work.
- ☐ Begin constructing your portfolio.

MAKE YOUR WORK THE STAR OF THE SHOW

"As a rule, conventions only become conventions if they work."
—Steve Krug

9. Tips for Creating a Digital Portfolio

Let's face it, you're going to need a digital version of your portfolio, but with so many options available you might be thinking 'what platform should I use?' The answer to this question is largely based on personal opinion and need, but here are a few considerations to think about before making your decision.

Do you need a website? This might come as a surprise, but not everyone does. Perhaps a PDF portfolio is all you need. The answer to this question largely depends upon the audience you're trying to reach. If promoting and sharing your work through a website is an expectation of your audience, then chances are good a PDF portfolio won't suffice. However, if your audience has no expectations of you having your own website, then perhaps a PDF version of your portfolio is a viable option for you to consider.

Creating a PDF portfolio is relatively easy and it's fairly painless to update. If you decide a PDF portfolio is the right direction for you, then take the time to create an interactive PDF which uses hyperlinks to navigate your document. I like to create a Table of Contents and hyperlink the titles of my projects to their corresponding pages. I also follow a web convention and create a hyperlink from my logo back to my Table of Contents to make navigating the document easier for the viewer.

Creating hyperlinks within a PDF document can be accomplished easily with Adobe InDesign and/or Acrobat and there are some easy-to-follow online tutorials you can watch if you're unfamiliar with this process. One last piece of advice is to try and keep your PDF portfolio under 10MB in size in order to prevent getting blocked by your target audience's email client when your PDF portfolio is sent by email. A good practice is to compress your images with Photoshop rather than relying on Adobe's 'Smallest File Size' preset, which optimizes images that exceed a predetermined pixels per inch value.

Assess your coding skills: If you determine you need a website, then you need to honestly assess your coding skills. Nothing can be more frustrating than getting into a website project only to realize half way in that you've bitten off more than you can chew. There are some easy-to-use website options out there that allow you to have a web presence but are designed to help you bypass some of the coding drama associated with building a website from the ground up.

- **Behance:** Behance is a platform created by Adobe to create and discover creative work. If you've purchased the Adobe Creative Cloud, then you automatically have access to Behance. Behance tends to be 'project-centric,' meaning the bulk of your customization efforts will be made at the project level, rather than creating a more traditional website experience.

- **Adobe Portfolio:** Adobe Portfolio is free if you've purchased an Adobe Creative Cloud subscription. Adobe Portfolio allows you to create a portfolio website by choosing one of their layouts and customizing the design. It also offers more advanced features like customized URLs, Google Analytics, Typekit fonts, and so forth. While Behance and Adobe Portfolio are separate services, they are designed to work together. Projects from Behance can be imported into Adobe Portfolio and vice versa.

- **Coroflot:** Coroflot is one of the longest running career communities whose mission is to connect creative talent with opportunities around the world. Coroflot offers free portfolio hosting and access to their job board. Having these two components under one roof makes it easy to apply for a job quickly just by clicking an 'Apply Now' button on the Job Description.

- **Wix and Weebly:** Wix and Weebly are easy-to-use website building platforms which offer free accounts, but charge clients more for features like removing ads, creating forms, storage space, bandwidth usage, and so forth. While Wix is larger than Weebly, both companies have a good reputation. Both platforms allow you to start with one of their prepopulated templates and then customize it to meet your needs. While Wix and Weebly offer similar services, there are distinctions between the tools they offer, how to add content, and the features included in their plans.

- **Squarespace:** Squarespace is an all-in-one platform for creating websites. Squarespace is similar to Wix and Weebly in many ways, but their templates have been professionally designed, responsive, and arguably of a higher quality. Squarespace has a 14-day free trial to let you test their platform, but then requires you to purchase a plan at the end of the free trial. Squarespace allows users to pay month-to-month or yearly, making it easy to start and stop service at any time. Month-to-month plans cost slightly more than yearly plans (~$4.00/month), but allow you to cancel your services at any time.

- **WordPress:** WordPress is a popular content management system that, like Square-space, helps you create beautiful and functional websites. WordPress is an open source platform and the code is open to customize and use. This allows developers to create tools and share/sell them to WordPress users. Open source platforms can sometimes be a double-edged sword; while you typically have lots of tools available, many of these tools are mediocre or poorly designed. Poorly designed tools can cause conflicts, poor performance, cross-browser conflicts, crashes, or lead to you getting hacked. WordPress is very flexible and customizable, but you need to be careful about the tools, themes, and plug-ins you use—make sure to read the reviews before installing them.

If you feel comfortable coding in HTML and CSS: If you feel confident using HTML and CSS then you might want to consider using a front-end framework like Twitter Bootstrap, Skeleton, Foundation, and so forth. These popular front-end frameworks are used for developing generic designs rapidly and allow you to customize your website more rapidly than designing a responsive website from the ground up. Another great advantage of using a framework is that the code is well-tested. Teams of developers have worked on the framework long before you've implemented it and in many cases have tested the framework on a variety of browsers and Operating Systems. One of the biggest drawbacks to using a front-end framework is that you need to be careful of code bloat when you begin customizing your website. As you begin to modify code and override default styles you can find yourself knee-deep in customizations. It's important to remember the DRY acronym (Don't Repeat Yourself) when working with a front-end framework—otherwise you'll have code bloat.

Creating your website from scratch: Typically, this is the least followed path because it can be one of the most time- and resource-consuming options. However, depending on what profession and job you are trying to enter it may still be a good option to consider. If you code your website yourself, then you'll still need to follow proper conventions, meaning you need to avoid using deprecated code, make sure to test your site in various web browsers and Operating Systems, and follow good coding practices.

It's exceedingly likely that you'll need to know HTML (content), CSS (style), and either Java or JavaScript (behavior) to make a website that will meet your needs. If you decide to code your own website, then your code becomes an extension of your crafts-manship, so be prepared to have your code looked at and evaluated. If you do it well, then coding your own website can be a real feather in your cap, but if your website is coded incorrectly then it may count against you.

> *"Your digital portfolio shouldn't look like there is no relationship between it and all of your other documents."*

However, one of the most positive aspects of creating your website from scratch is that your website will be uniquely yours. There's no template being sold to others that can cause confusion or dilute your brand—you're creating something original. If you do it well it can really make you shine! However, don't assume that just because your website looks good that the quality of your code will not be evaluated also. When you're finished coding your website it might be worth your time to go to W3C (validator.w3.org) and validate your code to make sure you've coded your website correctly. When you're able to establish a unique look and your website is coded properly, then the sky is the limit!

WHAT PLATFORM SHOULD YOU CHOOSE?

In a nutshell, you've got to choose the right tool for the job. Part of your decision about what platform you should use to build a digital portfolio will be determined by your target audience and the other part will be determined by your proficiency with code and ability to use the tools at your disposal.

Will you get called out for choosing to create a website where you've used Square-space instead of WordPress? Probably not. But don't forget that your digital portfolio is an extension of your branding and other design decisions. Your digital portfolio shouldn't look like you are simply highlighting your work with no visual relationship or connection between it and all of your other documents. It's important to remember that you are presenting yourself as a cohesive, total package rather than a la carte. Your digital portfolio needs to be cohesive with the other design elements and decisions you've made.

In addition to establishing consistency, there may be other considerations you might need to contemplate too. For instance, does your digital portfolio need to be responsive or optimized for a mobile device or tablet? If so, this consideration may eliminate several platforms from consideration. Does your digital portfolio need to be easily updated? If so, then you'll need to test various platforms and decide what platform makes this easiest for you. Do you need to be able to tag and filter work? Do you need search features? If so, then use this criteria to help identify the platform that best suits your needs.

By identifying and understanding your needs you're likely to be able to narrow your options considerably. Creating a digital portfolio can be quite an investment of your time and energy, so it's best to prioritize and identify your needs in order to future proof your digital portfolio for as long as possible.

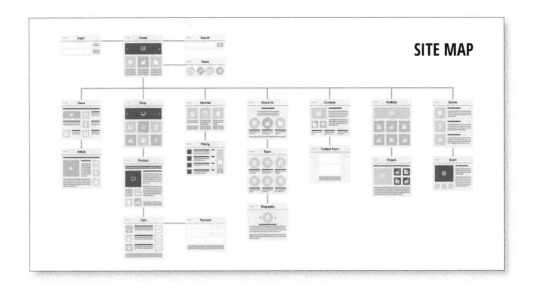

PLAN YOUR ARCHITECTURE FIRST

As you've seen first-hand, creating a plan before you begin working almost always makes the design phase more efficient—the same thing is true with designing a website. Your content needs to be tailored to an online environment rather than being simply copied and pasted in. Your pacing, flow of information, calls to action, and structure also need to be considered. If you think your digital portfolio is simply a digital version of your print portfolio, then you might need to adjust your assumptions.

Consider Your Content: People don't consume digital content the same way they consume printed, physical content. People tend to scan websites (rather than read them from top to bottom) and when they land on a website their eye path starts in the upper left corner and moves down and to the right.

Your website navigation should be placed at the top or left-hand side and calls to action should be placed lower and on the right-hand side. Big headlines and introductory paragraphs in a bolder and larger size can help pull people into your content. While people scroll on websites it's important to put your most important information above the fold at the top of your page. Finally keep your line lengths short and use columns of copy or shorter line lengths to make your content easy to digest.

What does your content have to do with your site architecture? Well, your content will likely be divided up into groups (or pages) that have an inherent relationship. You'll group similar types of content together to reduce the number of decisions your audience will have to make to get to the content they are looking for.

Categorizing versus Tagging: You might be tempted to create a section on your website titled 'Logos' and another section titled 'Videos,' but I would argue this may not be your best strategy because it may inadvertently create the perception that you are weaker in certain areas. If your website (and portfolio content) is divided up into too many sections then you risk creating a lackluster response from your audience after they've made numerous clicks only to discover you only have one video in your 'Video' section.

A better strategy (in my opinion) is to put all of your work into the 'Portfolio' section of your website and tag your content so it can be filtered easily by your audience. When all of your work appears on one page, your audience is less likely to notice that you only have one video and six logos and draw the conclusion that you're weaker in video because you have fewer video solutions in your portfolio.

Don't Drive Users too Deep: It's a good idea to try and limit the number of options (or clicks) a user must make to get to the content they want to see. Audiences typically don't want to 'drill down' into content through repeated clicking, and if they are willing to do so, the payoff better be worth the effort. User Experience (UX) data indicates what counts most is how easily the navigation is to use and delivering feedback to your audience, which indicates they are on the trail to finding the information they are looking for.

RESEARCH AND UNDERSTAND WEB CONVENTIONS

Users tend to scan websites and digital documents looking for highlighted keywords, meaningful headlines, short paragraphs, and lists, but only stop to read the content they are interested in word-by-word. This is one of many ways in which digital content is consumed differently than printed content. As such it's important to research and understand web conventions in order to design a good solution. Steve Krug, author of *Don't Make Me Think*, states, "Conventions are your friends," meaning there are conventions that work well because they are familiar to your users. Since users already know them well, they don't need an explanation or instructions. Take advantage of existing conventions in order to create a site that can be consumed quickly and easily. Below are a few selected web conventions for you to consider.

- **Scrolling:** Back in the mid-1990s people weren't used to scrolling for content, but this has since changed. While it's still advisable to put your most important information 'above the fold' you shouldn't feel like you need to squeeze content into this area. As long as you keep your audience engaged, they'll scroll down for more information. The kiss of death, however, is to make your audience scroll in all directions because your content has been presented in a format that is both too wide and too long.

> *"You've spent all this time picking your typefaces, establishing your brand, and developing your identity—don't throw all of this work out now simply because you're working in a digital environment."*

- **Accessibility:** Try and assess the needs of users by creating an accessible site. This may take a little extra effort, but in the long run accessible sites are easier and cheaper to maintain and if you needed further incentive—may rank higher with search engines by being SEO friendly.
- **Limit Choices:** Having choices to choose from is generally considered a good thing, but the more choices you offer, the harder it may be for your users to understand what it is you're trying to communicate. Studies show that having too many choices can lead to feelings of frustration while simpler solutions have a higher satisfaction rate. As such, don't overcomplicate your site with too many external links, navigation options, or calls to action that may lead to paralysis-by-analysis.
- **Consider Your Content:** Using dummy copy and stock photos to design your website often creates an aesthetically pleasing, but unrealistic result. Instead, build the design of your site around your content. Luke Wroblewski, author of *Site-Seeing: A Visual Approach to Web Usability*, argues that using dummy content and fake information in the web design process can result in 'potentially serious design flaws.' In short, a website with quality content will outperform a website with a nice layout, but subpar text. Make sure to build your website around the needs of your content rather than only making aesthetic-based choices from dummy copy.
- **White Space:** Use white space in your website design. Although many consider it a waste of screen real estate, it's essential in web design and according to designer Jan Tschichold, it should be "regarded as an active element, not a passive background." White space improves readability, hierarchy, and content prioritization and provides the viewer with areas of visual rest.
- **Be Consistent:** You've spent so much time picking your typefaces, establishing your brand, and developing your identity—don't throw all of this work out now simply because you're working in a digital environment. Be consistent in the ways you format your text and images and extend your brand to an online environment.

Consistency doesn't just pertain to extending your brand, it also applies to how you treat your visual elements. I'm always a little disappointed when I see a portfolio where the size of the images appears to have no connection to each other or where headers and subheads have been treated differently from one page to the next. In many cases these

> *"Don't position yourself as a jack-of-all-trades in your portfolio. Instead, highlight your strengths and demonstrate that you know what you're doing."*

inconsistencies disorient and confuse the viewer. Once you establish a system, whether it be a grid system, typographic system, or branding system stick with it and be consistent! If you need to make a change, then make sure the change gets applied universally throughout all your documents.

- **Focus Your Message:** It's important to identify your goals and use the content on your website to help focus your message. Resist the urge to post work or writing samples to show your breadth even though it may be tempting. For example, only include a blog on your website if the content will be relevant to the position you are applying for. Similarly, I occasionally see graphic designers include a 'Photography' or 'Fine Arts' section to their website. Unless this work is relevant to the position you are applying for and curated as rigorously as the other work in your portfolio, it should be removed. Don't fall into the trap of throwing all of your content to the wall and hoping something eventually sticks. It's far better to focus your message and keep things simple than it is to keep adding in additional content and fouling up your message.

- **Pace Yourself:** Pace yourself: Don't cram information into your pages, but look for opportunities to combine pages with lighter content together, while dividing pages with robust content up for greater consistency. Most students only need content for a Home/Index page, a Biography/About Me page and Portfolio page, but there are certainly exceptions to this. I've seen many students struggle with the content on their Home page because they feel it's repetitive with the content on their Biography/About Me page. In my opinion, it's better to merge two repetitive pages into one well-written page than to try to make a bigger website and spread your content too thin.

FOCUS ON THE WORK

It's exceedingly likely that your audience is going to your website to see your work and then if they like what they see, they want to get to know a little bit more about you—not the other way around. Make sure you emphasize the work on your website and highlight quality over quantity.

Websites make it easy to show lots of work because the medium doesn't function like other analog mediums. Slideshows, carousels, collapsible elements, downloads, and other tricks allow you to cram in more content than you would otherwise. Use discretion when choosing the content to put in your website because it's an easy medium to lose focus on your message and get caught up in 'coding tricks' instead. Just because you have content that *could* be put on a website, it doesn't mean you *should* put it on your website. I've been helping graphic design students create portfolio websites for a while now and I've seen a lot of photography work put into slideshows over the years. If photography work isn't relevant to the position you're seeking, then leave it out! Unless showing your photography work (or any type of work) helps you move closer to your goal, then don't muddy the waters by positioning yourself as a jack-of-all-trades in your portfolio. Instead, highlight your strengths and demonstrate you know what you're doing!

Similar to how you organized your print portfolio, think about the order in which your work appears and try to create a narrative or flow through the work in your portfolio. It goes without saying that you should put your best content above the fold, so when the audience clicks on one of your portfolio pieces don't use the top of the page to show your sketches. Even though the sketching process probably came first, don't feel like you have to use the page chronologically from the top to the bottom. Open with your money shot—your final solution in all its glory—and then show your process work (if relevant) as you scroll down the page. Ask yourself, "If my audience only sees one thing on this page, what do I want it to be?" and then make sure that thing goes in above the fold. This way your primary message gets delivered first and if it makes a good impression then you might pull them into your tertiary content.

You're going to want to use high-quality, optimized images of your work in your website. Many websites are 960 pixels wide minus a few pixels of padding, but it makes sense to take advantage of the full width (or a large area) of the page with your 'money shot' and then use your grid system to size other images of your solution, process work, sketches, and supporting text.

Nobody likes to wait for websites to load, so do yourself a favor and optimize your files to reduce their file size and help them load quickly!

Creating a sense of hierarchy on a web page is just as important as it is on a printed page, so don't lose sight of this as you work on your website. Templates make working in Content Management Systems easy, but don't forget about using white space to reduce visual clutter and to make your content easier to digest. At the end of the day, each page on your website should look like a designer who knows what he or she is doing has touched it. Using high-quality, optimized images will help pull your audience in, a good use of hierarchy and white space will direct them where to look, and well-written content will help you deliver your points quickly and effectively.

DIGITAL MEDIUMS AREN'T PASSIVE

Digital mediums aren't passive, so don't treat them as static content. Here are a few easy-to-follow tips that you should think about using on your website.

- **Hyperlinks:** Use hyperlinks to link to content and make sure to open content that isn't yours in a new window. For example, if you worked at an internship, then link to the company's website, but make sure to open the link up in a new window or tab. This helps the audience realize they are leaving your domain and entering a new area. It's particularly good form to let your audience know a hyperlink will open a new window by using a open new window icon in front of your hyperlink like this: "This is an example of hyperlinked ☑ text with an icon that indicates it will open in a new window."

- **Create a downloadable résumé:** There's no need to put your entire résumé inline on your website when it could be saved as a PDF document and downloaded easily. While you might want to highlight some of your biggest accomplishments on your website, putting your résumé content inline on your website can impede the hiring process because your document isn't as easy to share with others on a team. Make your résumé easy to find and download on your website by including it in your site navigation bar.

- **Promote your work:** Pretend for a moment that you've created a video, uploaded it to YouTube, and embedded the video in the portfolio page of your WordPress website. It takes me one click to go directly to YouTube where I can see exactly how many people have viewed your work. When I go there and see that your piece has received a total of 17 views, I suddenly get less excited about watching your video.

    You've got to promote your work! Not only is it a good Search Engine Optimization practice, but it helps you create a sense of momentum for your work. It helps create the sense that others are looking at your work already and that it's something worth looking at. Create thumbnail images that draw views in. Give your work irresistible titles. Use keywords that show mostly video results from Google, and integrate calls to action into your work. Allow others to embed your work on their websites and write and comment about it. Engage with viewers. Promote yourself!

    When I click on your link and I see you've followed these steps and have 1,500 or more views, then as an employer I'm starting to feel really good about you. It shows me that you don't just produce content, but that you understand how distribution and audiences work as well. It's easy to fall into the trap of being modest about your work and not wanting to promote yourself, but part of your job (like it or not) at this moment

DON'T FORGET YOUR CONTACT INFORMATION

in time is to stand out, not blend in, and put your work out there. While it might seem awkward at first, you'll soon get into a rhythm using your social media channels to drive traffic to your content.

- **Integrate calls to action:** Calls to action need to be eye catching and easy to spot. They also need to contain copy that makes people want to act. When writing a call to action begin with strong verbs (e.g., buy, shop, order, download, subscribe) and use adverbs (words typically ending in 'ly') more sparingly. You might use a call to action like "Contact me here with your questions" or "Download my résumé." Compare these statements to weaker calls to action like 'Contact me' or simply 'Résumé.'

- **Make sharing easy:** Since you're working on your website, make it easy for your audience to share your work by including social sharing buttons on each page of your website. These buttons provide an easy, one-click way to share content from your website as well as a visual reminder to your audience to share something they found interesting or helpful. WordPress has lots of social media plug-ins to choose from, so experiment and find a plug-in with the options you're looking for. Additionally, you can configure your website to support article pins to make it easy to share on Pinterest.

  Make sure to share your own social media profiles on your website. Many people like to give credit with @ mentions, so make your social media profiles easy to find in the header or footer of your website to help you build followers.

- **Use analytics:** Analytics are a way for you to monitor your content and see what's getting the most shares on social media. This information can also help you refine your content strategy and drive more traffic to your website. In a nutshell, analytics tells you who visits your website, how they got there, what they did once they landed there, and where they went afterward.

  Analytics can be used to get to know your audience better (where are they from, have they visited your website before, what web browser they use, and so forth). They can also record information about your audience's behavior like which of your pages are the most popular and how long the audience spends on your website. Finally, analytics can show you how your audience found you, who referred them, and what keywords your audience typed into a search engine to find you. After I go on a job interview I'll monitor my website analytics carefully to see what the employer looks at on my website, how long they spend on my website, and how many times they return to my website in order to gauge their level of interest in hiring me. I highly

If you are using a Content Management System, purchase a plan that allows you to use a custom domain name and then purchase a domain name for yourself. Don't go for the inexpensive options that force you to use a particular domain name, forced advertising, watermark your content, or provide limited templates or design options to choose from.

suggest that you install Google Analytics (analytics.google.com) on your website and monitor your website. Once you sign up you can enter in your website information and Google Analytics will create a small snippet of JavaScript code. You'll place this code on every page of your website and Google will begin collecting data on how the user engages with your site. You can access the results easily by using the Google Analytics interface after your data has begun being collected.

ACTIONABLE ITEMS
- ❏ Choose a format for your portfolio.
- ❏ Plan your site architecture and research web conventions.
- ❏ Use good Web strategies for engaging your audience.
- ❏ Purchase your hosting plan and register your domain name.

10. Social Media and Networking

by Diane Gibbs

Your social media platforms and online portfolio can create a stage for conversations to begin and relationships with people in the industry to grow. Social media can be a place to learn, meet others, and begin a dialogue with industry leaders and rising stars. Just like your portfolio, your social media channels create an impression and are perceived as a visual extension of you. In some cases your social media accounts create a higher definition snapshot of you because your posts reveal who you are, what is important to you, and how serious you take the industry you are trying to break into.

Students often present their portfolios to get hired, freelance, or apply to graduate school. These are big life-changing decisions, and following companies you are interested in on social media is a lot like dating before getting married. Before you make that big commitment to work somewhere you need to know the person/company better on a daily basis. Following someone on social media is a great place to start friendships and relationships that can lead to more long-term commitments like grad school, first job, etc.

Most businesses take hiring an employee seriously and they approach the hiring process as a long-term commitment. If you don't think they will look through your social media channels, then you are fooling yourself! Businesses look through the lens of social media to better understand what people (like yourself) are like. These channels give employers and graduate schools a clearer idea of the type of work you do, how often you are creating new work, and the quality of your work. These channels paint a picture of your consistency and growth over time, your personality, your attitudes, your responsiveness, humility, and quirks. It's important for you to edit and curate your social media content in order to better control the narrative of what you're really like professionally. As you know, interviews are a two-way street, and you should use social media channels to research the companies you are interested in as well.

> *"You want to create content that attracts the type of people you want to work with. Creating content needs to be something you do regularly and consistently."*

Virtually no one gets married after their first date, so why would a young professional expect to get a job offer or even an interview based on only sending their résumé to a prospective employer? Businesses want to know they are hiring someone that will be a good fit. That is where social media and networking come into play. Social media can be a bridge to developing a friendship and familiarity with companies and professionals you are interested in. These companies and professionals become a network of people you trust, and these friendships can lead to interviews and even potential freelance jobs.

If my company was hiring I would share this information with my network and tell them what type of person (and skills) I am looking for. I would ask if they know anyone who fits the description. I trust my friends to send me the names of creative individuals who will fit in with my company culture and the needs. When I receive recommendations, one of the first things I'll do is to look the candidates up online. If I looked at your profile online right now what would I find out about you? Would your social media posts make me feel better or worse about hiring you? In a nutshell, the more friends you have, the better your chances for getting interviewed because someone can vouch for you, but you must do your due diligence and curate your social media accounts.

How do you make friends online? You probably don't want to come across as a stalker or insincere. In some respects it is not about quantity (or how many connections you have), it is about quality relationships. At the same time you have to get your name out to a larger pool of people, so quantity is important too. There are social media accounts that claim to guarantee 10,000 followers if you pay a fee. These are scams and are accounts that are created by computers not humans. There is a difference between buying followers and gaining actual followers. You do not want to purchase followers. You want to create content that attracts the type of people you want to work with. Creating content needs to be something you do consistently (a minimum of once a week).

A few years ago, Rocky Roark had just graduated with a degree in graphic design but was having a hard time landing a position. He had made some great connections online and had some incredible illustration and design work in his portfolio, but finding a job was taking him longer than he expected. Instead of sitting around and worrying, he decided to improve his skills and began taking online classes and posting his

Colin Tierney: Making Connections & Highlighting Side Projects

Lettering artist and designer Colin Tierney owns and operates Tierney Studio, a design studio based out of Shepherdstown, West Virginia. Colin graduated with a Bachelor of Science in Graphic Design from Towson University located just outside of Baltimore, Maryland.

Q: How has social media and networking played a role in making connections, getting clients, and landing jobs?

A: Social media has been a game changer for me personally as well as professionally. The Internet has given me the opportunity to make digital companions that have turned into long-lasting friendships.

Every social platform serves a particular purpose, but when your profession is as niche as design—more specifically, hand lettering and calligraphy—it's easy to come across recurring peers willing to help, discuss, and support one another. When you have a community of people who are willing to help you grow, your work naturally becomes better. It's inevitable the clients will follow.

Q: How do you communicate your passion for our industry?

A: My passion for the design industry trickles down to helping people. I receive a lot of questions about my work, how it was created, and so forth. I've created a platform for people to reference, which provides lessons on hand lettering and calligraphy. I dubbed this platform Crayligraphy. Learning the art of beautiful penmanship becomes less intimidating when you base it around a marker. Crayligraphy is easier for the novice because they can emulate any style of calligraphy without the difficulty that comes with a pen nib or brush pen.

Q: What are things you did to help you grow your audience and exposure?

A: Consistency and sharing only my best work has helped me grow my audience. I'm aware of the quantity over quality shift as of late. For me, my work had to be the best if I were to expose the world to it. What I considered my best work at one time has significantly improved compared to the work I produce today.

www.TierneyStudio.com TierneyStudio TierneyStudio TierneyStudio

solutions on his social media channels. He was posting his work so consistently one of the employers he sent his résumé to noticed how active he was. The employer noticed Rocky's activity because he had built an online relationship with this person many months before he needed a job. The employer noticed how quickly Rocky was posting new work and said that he was impressed with the quality of his work. Rocky was given an interview and was offered a job. None of this would have happened if Rocky hadn't began conversations and online friendships with the decision makers and industry leaders where he wanted to work.

The strategy that worked for Rocky can also work for you. A great place to begin is by following the social media accounts of designers and creatives you admire, as well as people and companies you would like to work for. After following and regularly liking posts, begin by commenting authentically on these people's posts with thoughtful, clever, and intelligent comments that go beyond "Dude! That Rocks!" or "Beautiful!"

When the person replies to your intelligent observations, ask a question or begin an exchange with them (if it's appropriate to do so). You are building a friendship and they take time. Don't expect this individual to call you for an interview anytime soon, but you do want them to begin to recognize your name. It would be great if they see you are regularly commenting (not just for one week), but your goal is to come across as being thoughtful, intelligent, and consistent comment enough that they go to your profile and see something worth following in return.

You are building relationships with people in the industry, so comment, ask questions, and be sincerely interested in their work. By doing so you will begin to build a following. Then start sharing strategically themed content, new skills, and/or side projects. Make sure to be present, active, and responsive to the comments on your social media feeds.

SETTING GOALS FOR ONLINE ENGAGEMENT AND NETWORKING

Clarifying and defining your online profile will help you land more interviews in your final semester. At the same time your social media and networking goals need to be realistic and attainable. You don't want to get started and then suddenly feel frustrated or give up because you haven't reached an unrealistic goal like 10k subscribers or followers. Your goals should be consistent exposure, authentic connections, and solid leads within the industry.

Realistic goals start with understanding your available time to create posts, you also have to spend time researching and finding people and companies to follow. After conducting your research you need to spend time commenting and responding to comments on different platforms. You need to not spread yourself thin by posting on 18 different social networks, instead start on the platform where most of your ideal audience

> *"Long-term goals are made up of many short-term goals. Having someone who understands both where you are currently and where you want to be is critical to being able to make attainable and realistic goals."*

spend the majority of their time. After you get the hang of one platform and manage it well, add another platform. Try and work up to three or four platforms total. It can feel like a full-time job just to manage your social media accounts, so don't let it get out of control. Make goals for daily and weekly time spent on each platform and stick to your goals.

Online engagement is everything from liking, commenting, sharing, and responding. Networking is essentially getting to know people in the industry and having them recognize you by your work, your name, your social media handle, or by your comments. Networking gives you shared experiences to talk about if you run into the people you follow in-person and provides you with a foundation to work from.

In-person events are experiences you should plan to engage in as you grow your social media audience. You want to attend as many events as possible, but again be realistic and strategic by deciding which events will bring the type of people or companies you would like to work with. Identify upcoming events in your area or in the area you are planning to relocate to. Events like Creative Mornings, Dribbble meet-ups, and AIGA events can help you get your foot in the door. Schedule at least two in-person events during your final semester and come to the event ready to talk to people and meet lots of people. Make connections online before going to your first online event to make the evening more productive and comfortable. If you have a great conversation with someone, ask if they could look over your portfolio and give you feedback.

YOUR ONLINE PERSONA

You want to demonstrate you are serious about your chosen field and are ready to hit the ground running. At the same time, you want to show your personality and demonstrate what you value. Bob Ewing a lettering artist and designer in Indianapolis, Indiana started a lettering-a-day project back in September of 2013 and published a piece of work everyday for over 530 days.

From this exercise he was able to grow his audience, exposure, and obtain freelance work. He had a highly curated feed because of this project, but he also didn't want his feed to be inauthentic; instead, he wanted it to reflect his personal values. From

Zachary Smith: Social Media Trends and Other Advice

Zachary Smith is a lettering artist and illustrator based out of Brooklyn, New York. He started lettering in 2012 as a way to share his thoughts and vent his frustrations. He quickly grew a following which led him to join the Sevenly team in 2013 as a Junior Artist. In 2014, he started his own illustration and lettering studio, creating work for clients such as Coca-Cola, Popular Mechanics, Converse, West Elm, Urban Outfitters, Wells Fargo, and more.

Q: How has social media played a role in establishing connections and landing new projects?

A: For the first three years of running my studio, all of my work inquiries came through social media or word of mouth referrals because I didn't have a website or an agent who was representing my work.

Q: Zachary, back in 2012 you erased all of your content on Instagram and started a more curated feed. Why did you do this?

A: I noticed a couple of drawings I shared got more likes than photos of sunsets, so I decided to delete everything and start building up a portfolio. At the time, Instagram was new and wasn't really being utilized as a portfolio platform for artists. I saw an opportunity to grow a following that would hopefully turn into a career. I started getting recognized for my lettering and my following started to grow.

Q: How do you stage your portfolio pieces? With mock-ups that you purchase?

A: For now, I take all of my own photographs. I rarely use templates or mock-ups, as a personal preference. Most photos I take on my Instagram and website were shot on an iPhone with good natural lighting.

Q: What did you do to grow your audience?

A: When I realized the opportunity of growing an audience on Instagram, I wanted to learn how I could do that for myself. After studying what the most successful people were doing, I learned two things: they share consistently and their content has a consistent feel to it. I committed to showing up consistently and people noticed. My advice to anyone who's just starting out is to show up and be consistent. If you're making good work, people will find you.

Q: You have had huge success getting your work noticed on social media which led to work. How hard is it to keep this up when you are busy creating for clients?

A: As my business has grown, it has become increasingly more difficult to stay active on social media. My advice to anyone who's struggling to share on social media while balancing client work or a job is to embrace imperfection. When you let go of the expectations to be perfect, you're going to create more, share more, and land more work.

zacharysmithh.com 🅞 zacharysmithh 🅞 zacharysmithh 🅞 zacharysmithh

Top: Illustration and typography created for Be Outfitter. **Middle Left:** Artwork created for Be Outfitter. **Middle Right:** Contribution to the NPS 100 project by TypeHike. **Bottom:** Illustration and lettering for West Elm.

the beginning Bob made a conscious effort to make sure that at least one of his nine most recent posts on his Instagram feed would be a picture of his kids or family. If his audience unfollowed him because he posted a picture of his daughter then he decided it was for the best because his family was extremely important to him and he wanted his audience to understand that his family was a priority.

Similar to Bob's decision, it's important for you to identify the environment and company culture that's right for you. You'll love going to work every day if the company's priorities are similar to your own. It is easier to find this type of information by following the employees within the company. Additionally, it might be beneficial to follow the decision makers at the companies you are interested in. Look at what type of work they create, the types of posts they comment on and like, as well as how they spend their off time. Do you see them hanging out with the people at work? Are they doing things outside of work that you also like to do? Do they attend the same type of conferences you would like to attend? Are they positive and inspiring or bitter and unwilling to?

You must decide what's important to you and how to communicate these things to others. For example, if you are interested in lettering and creating logo-types from scratch, it might be a good idea to share your ideation process, sketches, then final solution on your social media platforms. It's important to demonstrate your passions and strengths, as well as your additional interests both inside and outside the industry, but keep your posts about outside interests (e.g., mountain biking) to a minimum while you are in the middle of a job search. Here are a few points to consider when using social media:

- **Are your posts positive or negative?**
  You are on a flight that's been delayed yet again and will now miss your connecting flight. Do you share your frustration online? We are in an industry where things often don't go the way we planned. Expressing frustration publicly signals to others your inflexibility to and an inability to see past a stressful situation.

- **Are most of your posts of friends and selfies or pictures of your design work?**
  Pretend I am an Art Director and have just gotten a résumé from you. I pull up your Instagram feed or Facebook profile and see mostly pictures of you and your friends. Your feeds should reflect your interests and passions. If you want to work at a branding firm, I would hope to see a large number of logos in your social media profile. If you are posting pictures of your friends that's fine for a private account, but is the account you are sharing with your potential employers going to end well?

  Look at the majority of your posts and determine whether you need to create a new account and make your old account private, or delete all your posts not related to your industry. That means pictures with friends, vacation photos, anything your

Hebah Abdelqader: Using a Strategy on LinkedIn to Make Connections

Hebah works as a Senior UX Product Designer in the R&D department at Bofl Federal Bank in San Diego. After graduating with a B.A in Emerging Media—Graphic design, she studied User Experience Design online and pursued side projects. She impressed potential employers by launching a self-initiated project called By Design, which explores how culture influences the way people problem solve.

Q: How has social media and networking played a role in making connections, getting clients, and landing jobs?

A: Once I started getting serious about my UI/UX career I decided to clean up and refocus my LinkedIn profile. I came up with a strategy based on the Six Degrees of Separation theory. I unconnected from anyone who was not in my field and started to send connection requests to my idols. I searched for influencers and thought-leaders in the design industry and tried to connect with them.

I needed a way to stand out and attract my recipients to accept my requests, so I designed an interesting profile image that would reflect my skill set without the users having to read my title. My image needed to be interesting enough to entice them to click on my profile link. Once I completed my profile, I was ready to look for work.

I highly recommend that you take advantage of LinkedIn's free 30-day premium account. It's definitely worth your effort because your profile will be ranked high, and it is likely to be viewed by top recruiters. As a result of converting my account to a premium membership, I got contacted by a recruiter, interviewed at Disney, and was offered a Graphic Design Imagineering position, all within the span of two weeks.

In my opinion, the Mutual Connections Hypothesis is real! A month into putting my LinkedIn strategy in motion I made two connections that blew my mind, Debbie Millman and Jessica Walsh. As I connected with more of my design idols, my profile started to get viewed by more and more people.

My last and most valuable advice is this: send your LinkedIn connect requests with a personalized message. I always accompanied my friend request with a private message thanking them for the impact their content has had on my career growth. More often than not, you will get their attention.

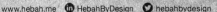

www.hebah.me   HebahByDesign   hebahbydesign   HebaH

Starting Side Projects After Graduation

by Diane Gibbs

Nick Brito graduated in 2016 from the University of South Alabama and got a job as a full-time designer for Mighty Advertising.

Nick had been interning at a local company during his final year and was going to continue working there part-time until he could find something more aligned with the type of design he wanted to be doing. Looking for a job on top of doing your senior thesis project is a lot of pressure and having this position really alleviated some of the pressure off of him.

In July after graduation, Nick decided to illustrate something positive from his day, every day, and made a commitment to do this until the year was over. He tried new styles and really used illustration in a way he had not done before. He was sharing it daily on Instagram and was gaining a following through using hashtags, being consistent in posting content, as well as regularly commenting on other designer's and illustrator's posts. By posting everyday and being active on the platform Nick's friends took notice.

One of Nick's friends and classmate was an intern at Mighty Advertising, an advertising agency in Mobile, Alabama where Nick lives. Mighty was looking for a freelance illustrator to help with a project. Nick would have not even been offered this had he not kept in touch with his classmates or had he not been showing his new knowledge and skills so frequently on Instagram. He agreed to work on the project and after completing the project was asked to stay on in a part-time position, which later led to a full-time gig with Mighty.

For Nick he wanted to show the type of work he wanted to be doing. He knew, "it's good to be versatile, but if you try and show a little bit of everything it will be harder for potential employers to see where you could fit in to their company."

Often students' confidence starts to wane as graduation gets closer, they start realizing they are competing against more than their classmates for positions. Nick's illustration project which was a self-initiated and self-driven side project helped build his confidence in himself and his work. He was able to tune out all the outside noise and focus on bettering his illustration and conceptual skills.

He will be the first to tell you his passion projects kept him motivated during his first, part-time design job. Nick said, "my personal projects allowed me to go home and create work I enjoyed."

target audience will not be able to relate to. Ask yourself if the post is inspiring, entertaining, or does it teach something? If the majority of your posts are of things that won't interest your audience you should delete them. Wipe your account clean and start over or create a new account and make your other account private. Then make sure to post curated content for the type of work you want to be doing.

- **How many of your last nine posts demonstrate a design strength?**

  Design as an industry is so large and varied that it may be beneficial to focus on an area or niche you are passionate about on your social media account. For example, Zachary Smith, a lettering artist and designer, really took this to an extreme and only posted focused content of his best skills. He was able to get his personality in by articulating his words and carefully editing his photographs. You can get an idea of who he is and what he likes from his social media channels.

- **How many of your last nine posts show you trying something new or developing a new skill?**

  No one is expecting you to be perfect. It takes a lot of guts to share your work online, especially when you compare yourself to people who have been doing it professionally for years. But how will you show your growth and progression if you don't put work out there? How will anyone know you are passionate about it and trying to improve your skills if you never show anyone? Social media can be an incredible platform for encouragement and growth. Don't get caught up making each post perfect, sometimes you have to hit publish and start the next creation.

SETTING YOUR SOCIAL MEDIA GOALS

It is important to know that building an audience, making connections, and starting relationships online is not something that happens in a weekend or even a month—it can take much longer. You must identify the key players you want to start relationships with and which platforms they use regularly. It's important to identify your social media goals, and little by little work toward achieving them. Here are a few questions to help you better articulate your goals.

- What kind of social media presence do you want to have in six months? In one year?
- How many followers and friends do you hope to have? How much engagement (shares, likes, comments per post) do you have in mind?
- What is your end goal in having this an online presence? Are you trying to sell products? Get more freelance clients? Teach workshops or use your experiences to help you get a full-time job?
- How do you want your audience to engage with you?

After you have stated your goals try to figure out what it will take to accomplish your goals. For example, if you have a goal of having your own business by age 35, you need to talk to someone who has started their own business. Identify a mentor and invite them to lunch to help you plan your next steps. Try and identify what your next steps might be.

Ask your mentor to help you create short-term and long-term goals. Short-term goals help you stay motivated and feel like you are making progress. Long-term goals reflect where you are currently and where you want to be and is a critical step in being able to generate attainable and actionable goals.

ASSESSING YOUR CURRENT SITUATION

Now that you understand what your goals are, you should evaluate your current social media situation. What area are you going to claim as your niche within your larger industry? For example, you love creating animal illustrations or maybe you like to create clever headlines with compelling photography, you will focus your social media content on this area of concentration. Having a focus area can and will change over time, so don't worry about picking a niche for a lifetime. This focus area should be something you excel in or something you are passionate about.

Austin Saylor, an independent motion designer who loves to animate lettering, said, "Your portfolio should reflect the work you want to do, not all of your work." Austin's online portfolio highlights projects dealing with animating lettering. This is not the only work Austin does but it's what he wants to focus on. By showing a focused goal you will signal to potential employers and clients the type of work you enjoy doing.

On page 161 there is an exercise to help you evaluate your voice on your social media platforms. Fill out your current stats on different social media platform. Write down all your accounts even if you have more than one on a single platform. Use the abbreviations to fill out the fifth column for the type of post you make: Photo (P), Video (V), or Animation (A). Sharing a link (S) or image/video from another account or resource, or text only post (T). Use the following abbreviations for the last column regarding the content of the post: Photo of finished work (FW), Process shots (PS), Question (?), Inspirational (INS), Information (INF), Venting (V), Entertainment (E).

Many posts' might use more than one abbreviation, so write down all of the abbreviations that apply to each post. In the last column mark whether the content you are sharing is original by circling the abbreviation. Repeat this self-assessment every week for a month. It will help you see which platforms you are gaining the most traction and allow you to focus on these for content, networking, and engagement. It will help you self-assess and identify trends in your social media posts.

EMPHASIZE YOUR STRENGTHS, PASSIONS, AND PERSONALITY

Joseph Carter-Brown: Relationship Building

Joseph Carter-Brown is a Front-End Developer for Unleashed Technologies, a hosting and web development firm in Columbia, Maryland. He recently shifted his focus from development to design, branding, and user experience (UX) strategy and calls himself a 'Devsigner.'

Q: What helped you land your job?

A: Having a solid understanding of web development was a big help. Many designers neglect to gain even a base level of knowledge of web development which hurts their ability to communicate with developers. Having a background in, and an understanding of 'devsign' means I know how to code, and design for the web. It means I know how to communicate my designs to developers in a manner in which they understand, so we have a good relationship and sense of trust which is crucial to solving problems together.

Q: What kind of research should someone do before applying and before an interview?

A: Research the company's philosophy, its values, and the types of clients they work with. Learn who you're interviewing with and the people who work there. Find a LinkedIn profile for the people you're interviewing with and try to see if there's something about them that you can connect with. At the very least read their biography on the company website.

Ultimately, your goal is to show you care. When you design a flyer, a logo, or a website you don't just sit in a vacuum and design, you think about who is going to use it, what they care about, what they want and need. Then you form your design decisions to align with those values. If you don't care about your user, or your customer, or your audience, then you're not going to connect—the same goes for a job or interview.

Q How has networking played a role in making connections with people in industry?

A: Networking has played a huge role, in fact I don't like using the word 'networking,' I prefer 'relationship building,' because that's really what you're doing. When people say it's not what you know but who you know, that's so true. While it'd be nice to think that simply applying to jobs blindly via online job boards is what gets you in the door, it's just not true! Companies want to feel comfortable with the people they hire, they want to know you are a good fit, genuine, not just putting on a show to get hired. This can't be completely gleaned in a one-hour interview. So having quality relationships with people who can vouch for you, especially when they are within the organization and industry you hope to work in, only helps build your name, reputation, and desirability.

www.anthonybrowncreates.com 🅞 abrowncreates 🐦 abrowncreates 🅛 www.linkedin.com/in/josephcarterbrown

Account Name	Platform	Number of followers	How often you post each week	Type of post (P, V, A, S, T)	Post content (FW, PR, INS, INF, V, E, ?)

Photo (P), video (V), animation (A), sharing a link, image, or video (S), text only (T), finished work (FW), process shots (PS), inspirational (INS), informational (INF), venting (V), entertainment (E), question (?)

INDUSTRY INVESTIGATION

A good place to begin researching a business or particular industry is by searching hashtags relative to your chosen niche. If you want to work in publication design then search social media the keywords like #publicationdesign, #magazinedesign, or #bookdesign. You are looking for people to follow and companies who have a solid body of work and actively posting. Here are a few tips to deepen your investigations:

01. Search social media using general, more specific, and niche hashtags.
02. Don't stop your search at social media. Search for groups in both social media and the Internet. Search for the topic within your local city on Slack (an app) and find a channel in your geographical area.
03. Find leaders at conferences or through conference sites, see who is speaking and/or leading workshops.
04. Discover new people to follow by looking in industry publications, magazines, annuals, and competitions.
05. Conduct multilevel research by going to websites, searching social media channels, or by conducting a Google search.

> *"To connect with more people in the design industry, you must generate quality content consistently, using proper hashtags, and post at times when your target audience will be online."*

Research ten leaders each day for five days. Choose leaders that inspire or are influences in your profession rather than arbitrary or random people. In addition, identify five companies each day who are doing the type of work you love. Finally, find five companies each day who are doing great work, but who work in a different discipline. From this list see who pops up in your social media feeds, investigate the hashtags they use, and look up keyword searches on Google. At the end of the five days you will have fifty industry leaders and fifty companies to pull data from. Create a spreadsheet and record whether these contacts are providing you inspiration (INS), information (INF), entertainment (ENT), and if they are a potential contact (PC).

The next step is to follow your new leads and identify which ones resonate with you. Keep recording the type of posts they make and add this information to your chart. If you comment on a post add this information into your spreadsheet as well. As a general rule, when you comment don't simply write a one liner of praise, but comment in a way that demonstrates your insights and intelligence. For example, if a color palette is interesting or their pen work complex, express your admiration of these details in full sentences using correct punctuation and spelling.

From the list you created, narrow your focus down to five leaders/companies who have inspired you and are doing the type of work you want to be doing. Research the leader or company on at least five different platforms and take screenshots of their profile pictures, biographies, last five posts, and last five likes. Make a note if they are posting original content or sharing someone else's content.

In your spreadsheet include the items below for each of the ten leaders/companies in each of the five different platforms: account name, person's name, person's company name, profile picture, biography, last five posts (take screenshots) and original content (O), sharing someone else's content (S), date of last post, engagement of their last post (likes, shares, comments), and the last five hashtags they've used. Your goal is to create a profile of these users so you can capitalize on this information later.

Select five of the following social media platforms (Facebook, Twitter, Instagram, YouTube, LinkedIn, Pinterest, Google+, Dribbble, and Behance) and write out answers to the five questions that appear on the following page:

Rocky Roark: Making Connections Before Graduation Pays Off

Rocky has worked as an in-house designer in a print shop, a branding designer, and a UI/UX designer. Currently he is based out of San Diego, splitting his time between his home-studio and a small one-person office at WeWork. He is a creative working as a freelance illustrator, branding designer, entrepreneur, and YouTuber.

Q: How has social media played a role in making connections and landing jobs?

A: When it comes to my last two design jobs, social media played a major role in getting in the door and landing them. With my first job, I hadn't even graduated yet and was already trying to find a potential job. I ended up following a lot of studios and the people who either worked there or even their founders. I would see tweets from certain people and instead of just liking or retweeting them, I'd respond to them. I realized the more you respond to people the more familiar they'll get with you.

Graduation came and went and I ended up moving in with my aunt in a rural town in Georgia. I slept on an air mattress and worked on my old iMac from her kitchen table. Instead of goofing off or sending out resumes, which I did a lot, I began to try to increase my skill set. I ended up joining an online education subscription site, Tree house, a week after graduation and began to take their courses to learn coding. I was zipping through the courses and each time I finished I would get a badge and was prompted to share my progress on social media and I shared every badge I received. The best part of all that sharing was some one was watching.

A few days in I had received over 25 badges from Treehouse. I remember checking out Twitter one day and seeing the same guy I had been talking to months ago had just gotten back from a conference in California. I decided to just send him a direct message and see how the conference went. Later that day, the guy sent me a message and said the conference was a blast, and he'd love for us to meet up next week and have lunch. "I'll have our project manager get in touch with you and set up a date and maybe we can find you a spot in the company!" All of that hard work and time spent on social media paid off and a week or two later I was starting at my first real design job.

www.RockyRoark.com rockyroark www.youtube.com/c/RockyRoark RockyRoark

Doing Your Research Works

by Diane Gibbs

Elaina Mastrilli, one of my students who graduated in May of 2017 with a degree in Graphic Design from the University of South Alabama. She took my Design for Social Media class in the spring of her junior year and applied the things she learned which I am sharing with you in this chapter plus a lot of effort and was able to secure a position in a new city before she graduated.

The semester started of with the students defining goals for their life and careers. I ask my students to investigate the cities they want to live in and dive into the design firms, agencies, and in-house opportunities in these cities. Because without a clear destination you will never reach your goal. In this research Elaina found a company she was already following and a fan of their products and services.

Elaina researched everything she could about the company. This was not a 15 minute endeavor, it takes time to dig into a company's history, read blog posts, watch videos, and study their social media posts on multiple platforms. She also had realistic goals of wanting to work for this company, because they were in a growing phase. Instructables is a young company

that began in 2006 out of a Lab at MIT and was expanding its team in 2017.

From her research on the company, Elaina realized that Instructable's values aligned with her own. She tailored her portfolio to match the type of graphics Instructables was using. She included things in her portfolio she knew would be required for the position she was applying to, for example, social media campaigns, advertisements, videos, and identity work.

By looking at the company from an analytical perspective, Elaina said she "paid attention to trends they used to promote specific content, and made notes about what they were doing, and what I felt could still be added. I think this helped prepare me for the interview because I was specifically asked to comment on their current social media contest campaigns, and what I would do if given the chance to work on them. I felt that by having prepared specific examples I was able to show my commitment, innovation and value to the company." Her knowledge gained from her research positioned her as intelligent and relevant. It clearly worked because Elaina now works for a San Francisco company on the Instructables team.

Profile Questions

01. How often are they posting original content and on which platforms?
02. What day and time are best for this person to get maximum engagement and exposure?
03. Which type of content is getting the most engagement? (original finished work, process shots, quote, question, other people's content they are sharing.)
04. Which platform/channel gets this person/company the most engagement?
05. Which hashtags are they using for their posts?

My students use this exercise to help discover companies they would love to work for. One of my students, Elaina Mastrilli, followed these exercises during the spring and summer of her junior year. By the following spring she understood one of her dream company's personality, mission, and how to reach them. She also understood what skills they were likely to value and strategies she might take to get noticed. Her passions, interests, and skills were similar to the company's and because she followed them for a long period of time, she knew she'd fit into the company culture well. Her research allowed her to tailor her portfolio, résumé, and social media profiles to help Instructables get to know her work. She made it easy for them to say, "We'd like you to come to work for us" through the curation of her portfolio and social media accounts to communicate her entrepreneurial and creative spirit. Elaina landed an interview over spring break and was offered a job with Instructables in San Francisco—the city where she wanted to live.

CREATING CONTENT TO ATTRACT THE TYPE OF JOB YOU WANT

To connect with more people in the design industry, you must generate quality content consistently, using proper hashtags, and post at times when your target audience is online. You must also commit time each day to commenting on other designers, illustrators, and animators posts.

How do you know what content will generate the type of engagement you're looking for? By creating original content or sharing someone else's content you can test your audience to see what type of posts are most liked or commented on and which types either increase or decrease friends/followers. Before you start creating original content, you should know your audience and research what they like and share. You want people to recognize you by your posts, your name, and your work. You want them to follow you because you create or share content that inspires, informs, or entertains people within our industry.

You are probably asking yourself what makes a successful post or a successful campaign on social media? You first need to identify and create a series, theme, or topic you can create content around for a specific length of time—remember you want to showcase your creativity and originality. Many of the things that make a successful post also make a successful and engaging social media ad campaign. There are some types of content that perform better on certain platforms and some platforms want you to upload native files for best exposure. For example, Facebook's algorithm rewards people who upload videos to their platform more than sharing a YouTube video. In addition to what makes ad campaigns successful, here are a few other tips to include in your posts.

- Photos using depth of field and a clear focal point (let there be a hero).
- Let the images feel like they're a slice of your life, well composed and photographed, with your piece as the hero.
- Use colors, contrast, and visual elements to connect multiple posts together.
- Don't use a lot of text in your posts. People don't use social media this way. When you do use text make sure it can be read at small sizes and make sure there is a call to action that's clear and concise.

Think of all the different types of content you consume: movies, videos, articles, images, lifestyle images, links to products, product reviews, and so forth. The list is endless. What kind of content could you create? Type up a list of content ideas and next to each write two things: 1) Whether it is an article you will write, an image you will create, a video you will shoot, an animation you'll make, or a link you will share. 2) Who is the target audience? The goal is to choose a topic broad enough to allow you to create an ample amount of content.

Get busy creating! Before you post for the first time you should have at least five pieces completed and ready to post at a moment's notice. Show your first five pieces to a few people you trust who will give you their honest opinion about the quality of your work. Ask them if your theme/topic is easily understood and repeat this process again, showing the people you trust your older posts with newer posts so your critique feedback will be more focused.

POSTING CONTENT (FINALLY)

Now that you have your first five posts vetted by someone you trust, you are ready to post. Look back at your investigation spreadsheet and find a day and time when most of your industry leaders/companies are online and create your post during these peak hours. Think of the time zone in the place you are wanting to move. Here is a trick, post five minutes before or after the hour or half hour to catch people as they are waiting for a meeting to start or for one to end.

Go back to your spreadsheet and see which three platforms your audience uses the most, this should be easy to find. If their last post was eight months ago, they're not on that platform regularly enough. Start with two platforms at first and work your way to posting on three platforms as you gain more confidence. Post native, meaning go to the platform and post there instead of using something like Instagram's ability to share onto other platforms—often these are just text links and won't catch people's attention.

Finally, use hashtags. Hashtags are general terms or specific terms used for searching for content on certain topics. Make sure to always use at least three: one general hastag (#illustration), one more specific but used by less people than the general hashtag (#bunnyillustration), and finally a hashtag used by only you (#gibbsbunnies).

CHAPTER REFLECTION

How can you make a good impression if you haven't investigated the messages you are sending on your social media accounts? How can you know what will catch the attention of someone you are trying to make a positive impression on? Every aspect of design starts with research. The better you understand yourself and your audience the better you can cater the messages you create to reach that audience. You now have the knowledge to know where to spend your time and energy instead of spinning your wheels and hoping something sticks. Having a strategy to highlight your strengths, passions, and personality is critical to you communicating the type of designer, employee, and team member you will be. Use the tricks used in this chapter to create relationships with people in the industry who will support you, vouch for you, and when the time comes even possibly help you get an interview.

ACTIONABLE ITEMS

☐ Identify a list of possible companies that possess the type of job and environment that appeals to you.

☐ Clarify your message, values, and personality you want to communicate on your social media accounts.

☐ Find three to four social media platforms to dedicate time on: posting content, commenting on other's posts, and responding to comments.

☐ Dedicate time each week to respond to posts you resonate with, making new connections and starting conversations when appropriate with people in the industry.

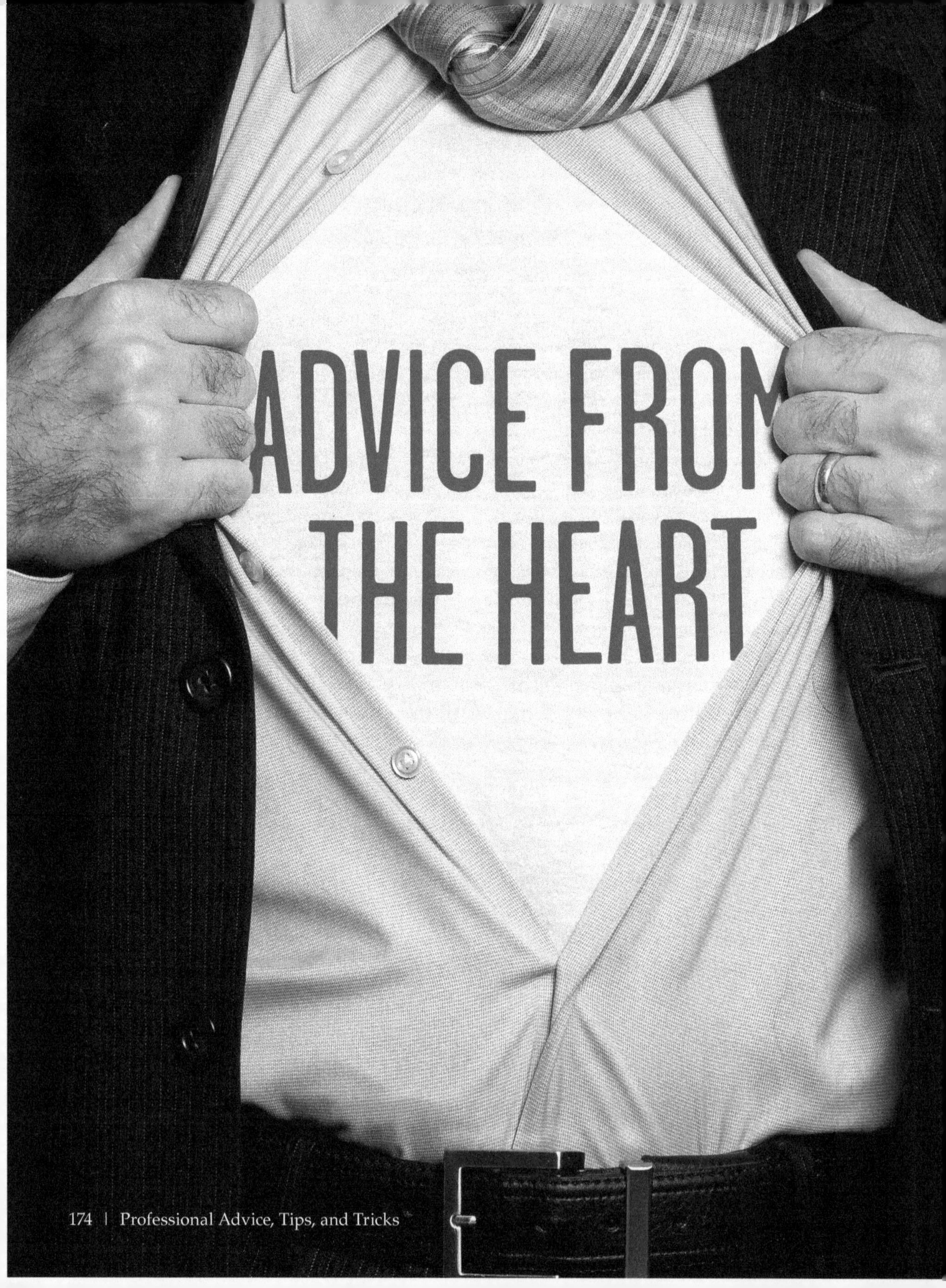
ADVICE FROM
THE HEART

11. Professional Advice, Tips, and Tricks

by Diane Gibbs

After interviewing designers and illustrators week after week, I have made lots of friends and learned a lot. I am so happy to share with you some designer insight on everything from interview tips to harnessing the power of social media and portfolio sites. This chapter is jam-packed with insights from some of the industry's up-and-comers, movers, and shakers. The people featured in this chapter have generously given their time and energy to answer questions to help you create a portfolio and an online presence to help you present yourself as the creative you want to be.

Take time to dig into the following stories and their professional backgrounds. Many of the following people have been featured on my podcast, Design Recharge, and you can go to RechargingYou.com to watch episodes. These professionals have shared their social media handles and I encourage you to follow them and comment on their posts. Reach out to them and tell them what their story meant to you and how you applied their insights to your portfolio.

It gets hard to balance it all: school, work, building a website, uploading to social media, reaching out for interviews, and so forth. Don't give up. When it gets tough, reach out to your professors and classmates, the design community, and try to keep making progress—one step at a time.

These designers' areas of focus range from User Experience and User Interface designers (UX/UI), illustrators, branding experts, publication designers, web designers, product designers, lettering artists, type designers, etc. I've found these people to be humble and willing to share, they push themselves (and their abilities) hard. They have struggled and overcome numerous obstacles. These people make the world richer through their work and their passions. I am in awe of them and I am so happy to introduce you to them over the next few pages.

Bethany Heck

Executive Design Director of Video, Data and Audience Engagement

Vox Media

Bethany earned her BFA in Graphic Design from Auburn University in 2010, a very print-focused school. She cultivated an interest in web design in junior high and adapted what she learned from traditional, design fundamentals to the digital realm. The web work has led Bethany to jobs in app and product design.

Q: **Are there any student projects you have in your portfolio? If so what makes them special that they remain in your portfolio? When would you replace a student piece?**

A: The Eephus League is still in my portfolio, since it's transitioned out of being a student piece, and I have five other student projects I've left in because they were fun to do and the work still holds up. They also show a type of design or an aesthetic I might not get to do on a regular basis, like the newspaper redesign or the Lou Dorfsman poster I made (which gets ripped off a fair amount!) I try not to highlight them but I like having them there. Good work is good work.

Q: **What are a few things you did or that were in your portfolio that aided in you landing this job?**

A: My portfolio has strong work in a variety of mediums. My portfolio pieces show that I can do branding, print design, web and product design. The portfolio site I designed also allows me to write in-depth about each project which is a skill I look for now in the people I'm hiring. If a designer can't

show any critical thinking about why they made certain choices, or if they can't show any understanding of how they pursue designing for a specific audience or user base, that's a huge problem.

In terms of projects that helped me land work, the Eephus League was a huge one. It began as my final student project and through Kickstarter it's now a small business for baseball scorebooks and merchandise and a website. When I first got out of school, being able to say I designed and built a website for a small business where I produced well-designed physical objects en mass was obviously a showstopper.

Q: **How do you present multipage documents in your digital portfolio?**

A: I present them as spreads if it's print work and as individual screenshots if it's web work.

Q: **What pieces do you include in your portfolio, no matter who the client? Do you cater portfolios for different employers?**

A: The Eephus League, my work on Power BI, and usually the work I did at IBM, depending on the employer. I adjust what I show depending on who the audience is, in the same way you need to write a unique cover letter for every position you apply for. You have to translate what you've done in the past against what you think this person wants out of this role in the future.

Top: *Microsoft Power BI allows users to take mounds of data and transform them into beautiful interactive visuals and reports.* **Middle left:** *The Eephus League digital magazine.* **Bottom left:** *Microsoft Power BI desktop screen creating clarity for users by introducing a second typeface.* **Bottom right :** *Lou Dorfsman student poster project.*

www.heckhouse.com   eephusleague   heckhouse

Matt Vergotis

Creative Director

Verg

Matt is from the Gold Coast, Australia and has been self-employed for the past nine years operating as Verg. He specializes in Corporate Identity and Brushpen Lettering. He moved from Australia to London in 1999, and began his job search by going to a few recruitment agencies that focused on the creative industry. When interviewing Matt made sure he was on point, well presented, and had his portfolio up-to-date and looking good.

Q: How do you show ideation and process in your portfolio? If you were hiring a designer to work for you full time, do you want to see ideation and process in their portfolio?

A: I love to see ideation and process! It tells the creative story helping someone to understand how you got from A to B. This is usually where the magic happens, so to be able to see and understand the thinking and process behind a creative's design gives you an insight into their creative mind and skill set. For me, showing tidy, well-photographed sketches, concept methodology, and construction mechanics are all interesting stages of the process.

Q: How has social media played a role in making connections and landing jobs?

A: Social media has been paramount in the success of my business. Love it or hate it, it's a valuable tool if you want to gain exposure. It

will help you broaden your clientele—even on an international scale—that would otherwise be difficult to do. When I started my business I was invisible. No one was contacting me about work. Becoming active on social media changed that, and my clients now recognize my work.

Q: What three characteristics, skills, or personality traits do you relate to your success?

A: It's definitely a mix of determination and patience. I have a little mantra I use when surfing one of the best (and most crowded) waves in the world which can also be applied to everyday life. It's the three P's. Position, Proactivity, and Patience.

First and foremost you have to be in the right position, if you're not in the right position you will never ever get a wave. Position yourself where the waves are breaking. Second, you have to be proactive to stay in the right position. Don't drift away or give up when other people crowd your position or when the current gets hard to paddle against. And finally, be patient, don't expect results immediately. If you concentrate on those first 2 P's, your opportunity will come. You will get your wave. Staying patient helps you enjoy the process and take in the beauty. It keeps your mind where it needs to be when your wave rolls in. Then take off and enjoy the ride of your life!

Top: Matt created a unique look by printing the brewery logo on all cans and then a label was adhered to communicate the style of beer. This enabled the brewery to cut costs by only printing one can design. **Middle left:** Final sketch for Black Hops. **Middle right:** A wall outside the Black Hops brewery. **Bottom:** Matt created this responsive logo for the Earl of Leicester Hotel. Responsive logos have multiple versions and adapt to the amount of space available.

www.verg.com.au   mattvergotis   VERG   vergadvertising

Von Glitschka

Creative Director
Glitschka Studios

Von is principal of Glitschka Studios, a small boutique design firm located in the Pacific Northwest. His diverse range of illustrative design has been used by some of the most respected brands in the world. He creatively collaborates with ad agencies, design firms, in-house corporate art departments, and small businesses to produce compelling visual narratives.

Q: What advice would you give someone trying to break into a career in illustration?

A: Learn how to design too because you need both to survive in today's market. I'd also tell a designer who has no interest in becoming an Illustrator they still need to draw, otherwise they won't be able to create certain types of work.

Q: What would you tell someone never to do during their first year on the job?

A: Not ask too few questions. Be curious. Don't worry if someone uses a term you don't know. Ask them to explain. If you aren't completely sure what something means, ask! Most of what you will learn in your career rarely comes from you setting aside time to learn it. You'll learn more through observation and asking questions along the way, so get used to it!

Q: What is something you notice about a designer's portfolio at first glance?

A: If they can draw or not. You automatically limit your creative potential if you don't utilize drawing as part of your creative process. There is a finite amount of aesthetics you can achieve without drawing and a far greater range if you utilize an analog drawing methods within a digital work flow. Drawing is probably more important now than it's been before.

Q: What is the one piece of advice you would give a student as they prepare their portfolio?

A: Show how you think—not just your final solution. Creative directors need to know you can problem solve and that has very little to do with grid layouts and elegant design. It has to do with taking raw information and organizing it. A good way of showcasing this is to include a sketchbook. Show thumbnails along with a mark you developed. Saul Bass said it best when he said, "Design is thinking made visual," show that you can think.

Q: How many résumés do you think the average student might send out before they land a job?

A: I have a friend who is a talented Creative director and he sent out 60 résumés and only had two phone interviews—neither went anywhere. Another friend was discouraged over this, so two years ago, I applied to over 25 positions to see if I could get a bite, and guess what? I never heard back from them and one of the positions I even had two people from the company recommend me. Companies are so inundated with applicants this is the new normal. You just can't give up. You've got to keep trying to make it happen.

Top: A small town brewery inspired by the subculture of Rock-a-Billy and Hot Rods has been embraced in the land of Rednecks. ***Middle right:*** Von created a strong and sophisticated brand identity for Big Ass Fans that is noncompromising and helps them continue to grow. **Left:** History inspired this small company's brand identity and packaging. Photo by Matt Swain.

Dustin Lee

Owner

RetroSupply Co

Dustin is the owner of RetroSupply Co. They create historical textures, brushes, templates, and other items. He earned his first real job in design the hard way through hard work, networking, and determination. Even though these are admirable traits, Dustin believes the best approach is to do work you're excited about, document your process, and build a platform.

Q: What personality traits do you possess that relate to your success?

A: I try to be myself. I didn't get into design because I love a good brochure (did anyone?) I love kitschy packaging and old-school copywriting. I bring my love of that to what I do.

Q: How much should someone know about a company and what they do before interviewing or even applying for a job?

A: Researching a job you don't much care for is a prescription for misery. Think about organizations you love and consume their work. Interview with those organizations and other companies who are like them. Your excitement about the work will show. You'll have great ideas to bring to the table and you'll find your job more fulfilling.

Q: Many students struggle with confidence and imposter syndrome. Have you ever struggled with this issue?

A: Yes. I've struggled with both, and I still feel like an imposter. I don't know if you ever get over it. I decided I wasn't going to spend my life waiting until I was sure I was 'a proper' designer. Forget about being an imposter! We're all imposters! Make the things you love. Be good to your customers. Share your work.

Q: What do you think when people say, "It's all who you know?"

It's true. Who you know makes a big difference in how successful you are. But most people have it backward. Make interesting work and share it. That will almost always result in relationships with people who can help you.

Q: What is something you notice about a designer's portfolio at first glance?

A: Curation. Stephen King has a great quote: "Kill your darlings, even when it breaks your egocentric little scribbler's heart, kill your darlings." When a design piece doesn't fit but it's added as filler, it can ruin the magic of the rest of the work.

Q: Do you want to see process work in a portfolio?

A: It's not necessary, but it can sometimes help. I prefer to talk to a potential employee on video or in a meeting.

www.retrosupply.co getretrosupply RetroSupplyCo retrosupply

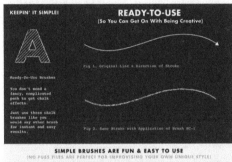

Top left: The cover image for a pack of digital chalk brushes for Adobe Illustrator. **Middle left:** Explanation PDF that comes with every brush pack to explain how to install, how to use, and a detailed description (with visual examples) of the actual brushes in the pack. **Bottom left:** Nighthawk is a retro-inspired font and this image is one of a few preview images which aids the customer to see how the font can look in use. Well-designed preview images make all the difference in communicating a product's abilities. **Right:** Roaster is mono-line font with a hand-lettering feel. This preview image is used on Pinterest to show how the font can be used, and drive customers to the website.

Nikki Villagomez

Creative Studio Director

Dixon Hughes Goodman LLP

Nikki received her BFA in Graphic Design from Louisiana State University. After graduating, she worked in New York City as an in-house designer and later as a freelance designer in South Carolina. Nikki taught Graphic Design and Typography at the University of South Carolina. She was offered a position as Senior Designer at Dixon Hughes Goodman LLP in Hudson, Ohio, and after two years was promoted to Lead Designer, then Manager and now Director of the Creative Studio at the firm's headquarters in Charlotte, North Carolina. Nikki is known for her side projects, where she combines photographs of typography in different cities and writes about how culture affects typography and design.

Q: What is one of your pet peeves about designers who are fresh out of school?

A: A lack of engagement. Be involved, always be ready to learn and show enthusiasm for the work you are doing.

Q: What kind of research should students do to get to know about a company before connecting with them online?

A: Find out what their mission statement is and how this statement resonates with you. Look into their 'About Us' page and see how you fit in and what, if any, aligns with you. If you get an interview, make sure to ask about what your day-to-day job will be like.

Q: What would you tell someone never to do during their first year on the job?

A: Don't be close-minded or go into your first job with preconceived notions of what it is going to be like. Be open to new ideas, change, and establish new relationships.

Q: How many résumés do you think a student might send out before they land a job?

A: However many it takes! I don't think there is a magic formula here. Finding a job that's a good fit takes a lot of patience and persistence. If your résumé is far-reaching across multiple states and regions, there might be more opportunity to find something quickly compared to looking for a job in a small town. Be willing to relocate if you can.

Q: What is something you notice about a designer's portfolio at first glance?

A: I notice there are a variety of typefaces and colors used. It's easy for students to fall into a safety zone with one or two typefaces and a specific color palette because it worked well for one project in the past. I like to see a variety of colors and typefaces used throughout their portfolio.

www.nikkivillagomez.wordpress.com nikki_vz ⓘ nikki_vz

CULTURE+TYPOGRAPHY
how culture affects typography

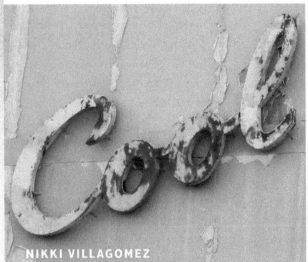

NIKKI VILLAGOMEZ

Top: Nikki has been writing a blog about how culture affects typography for several years. She travels around the United States speaking on this topic and her book, *Culture + Typography*, is a summary of her travels.

Bottom left: Nikki also has a passion for manhole covers, documenting them in different cities. She recently created a poster with 40 manhole covers from all over the world, this one from Albuquerque was part of that poster. **Bottom right:** While visiting Boise, Idaho this mural captured Nikki's attention.

Johnny Gwin

Creative Pilgrim—Advertising Art Director

1 Horse Design & Consulting, Deep Fried Threads, & Deep Fried Studios

Johnny graduated from the Portfolio Center in Atlanta and opened his own advertising agency in Mobile, Alabama. He partnered with two other creatives at Hummingbird Ideas and worked as an Art Director and Designer for many years. Recently, Johnny has gone out on his own and is doing design and content creation while producing and running Deep Fried Threads (an apparel and merchandise brand) and Deep Fried Studios where he is a podcast host. In his free time, he cofounded a coworking space called Container Yard with his wife in his hometown of Mobile, Alabama.

Q: What advice do you have for students as they prepare to enter the workforce and look for employment?

A: 1. Be bold. Think 'too' big.

2. Show me, don't tell me.

3. Work to become a craftsmen, and prove it.

4. Design and communicate like a storyteller.

5. Develop skills to be able to connect and understand others, especially people that don't look, talk, and think like you. Embrace the power of empathy.

6. Start showing your portfolio early in your studies and job search. Show your work to anyone that will look. Creative Directors can be an arrogant bunch of know-it-all's. Show your work to enough of them and you will know exactly what we are looking for.

Ask them how to make your work better for each campaign and we can't help ourselves, we'll tell you how to make it to our liking.

7. Realize that your portfolio is always a work-in-progress. It's never finished.

Q: What advice you would give a recent grad as they prepare their portfolio?

A: Start strong! Show your work in order from best work to least. While an interview seems like you are being judged on your talents and skills, you need to interview your possible future boss and coworker. Include a piece in your portfolio that is a 'litmus test' for the interviewer. Have a project that you loved making in your body of work, even if you're told not to include this piece. If your interviewer loves your 'test' piece, you might have found your mentor and your creative home.

Q: How do you show process work in your portfolio? Do you want to see ideation and process in a candidate's portfolio?

A: I love to see sketch books and idea books. Polished portfolios are a must. To me sketch and idea books show the 'real you.' Show me how you process information, dream, solve problems, communicate concepts, and search for 'what-ifs.'

johnnygwin.com   deepfriedstudios.com   thejohnnygwin   johnnygwin

{ MUSIC *for* BENCHES }

Top: *Music for Benches, a not-for-profit project for a concert series raising money for public benches in Mobile, Alabama.* **Middle:** *Posters designed for El Cantador, an Americana traveling band. Johnny's goal was to create posters people would steal off the wall.* **Bottom left:** *A logo for Nickel & Dime Records.*

nickel & dime records

Drew Hill

Creative Director
Element Three

Drew is a Creative Director at Element Three, a full-service marketing agency in Indianapolis, Indiana. He started his career in 2000 after deciding to follow in his father's footsteps to pursue a career in advertising and design. Drew is the co-owner of Inch x Inch, a nonprofit button club that supports youth art education.

Q: Do you prefer looking at a digital portfolio or print portfolio?

A: Ideally both, but if you can only invest time in one, I'd choose physical. While there is a level of savviness that comes with presenting a digital portfolio, you can't cover a table with an iPad. There is something to be said for being able to see the full breadth of some one's portfolio spread out in front of you. You can see their work in a broader scope, compare work side by side, and jump back and forth between projects with ease.

Q: What would you advise someone not to do in their first year on the job?

A: Don't sit back and wait for the opportunities to come to you. Take charge of your destiny and make your own opportunities. In your first year you'll most likely feel like you're just there to execute other's work. You can combat this by trying to add something to the work after you've completed the initial task. Maybe someone will like your suggestions, or maybe they'll trash them—who knows. At the very least you'll have exercised your skills while demonstrating that you aren't just a pair of hands.

Q: What helped you land your current job?

A: 1. Have a social media presence. When Element Three (E3) reached out to me, it marked the first time a job opportunity was presented to me on a social media platform.

2. Step outside your comfort zone. My background was in traditional advertising, while E3 was known for digital marketing. Even though it wasn't a perfect fit, I saw an opportunity to use my skill set in a totally new way. Don't be afraid to try something new, or step outside your comfort zones.

3. Have a unique physical portfolio. While interviewing, one of the very first things everyone wanted to see was my portfolio. I hand built an aluminum case and made it to look like a repurposed road sign, this definitely helped break the ice. Show off! Coming fresh out of school, you have a luxury that working professionals don't, you've never had to work with clients. It's a magical time in your career where you can do whatever you want. I love seeing work that provides a unique glimpse into someone's creative thinking and style. It's a purer representation of the designer, unsaddled from bureaucracy and a client's tweaks and opinions. So go on and flex because after a few years you'll be expected to have a book full of real work.

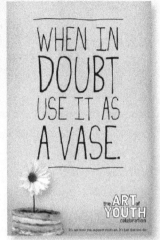

Top: *Poster campaign for The Art of Youth Celebration.* **Bottom:** *Branding and Packaging for Inch x Inch, a nonprofit monthly one-inch button club that supports national and local educational youth art programs.*

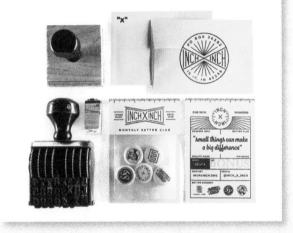

Scotty Russell

Freelance Lettering Artist and Illustrator

Perspective Collective

Scotty works as the lead web designer and graphic designer for the IDEX Corporation, but his passion for drawing led him to start his own side project called Perspective Collective. He uses this platform to encourage other designers and illustrators and get freelance projects that focus on his talents and strengths. Scotty uses Perspective Collective as a platform to combine his love for art and design.

Q: How has social media and networking played a role in landing jobs?

A: Let's be real here, Instagram changed my life. Sharing my art and learning how to utilize the platform properly opened a world of opportunities. I began by being consistent, engaging with the community, while adapting to the platform as it changed. This approach led to an engaged audience and serves as a mini portfolio where most of my freelance work comes from.

Networking has been pivotal in building connections and landing jobs. I build relationships with people and things grow out of that, I don't expecting anything in return. Just getting uncomfortable and putting yourself out there in front of the people you want to brush shoulders with is nerve wracking but it's necessary.

Q: Many new designers struggle with confidence issues. Have you experienced this before?

A: Not only have I dealt with this before but I deal with it everyday. While I'm confident in my abilities as an artist, there are still plenty of times I second guess myself or feel like a phony, especially when I have to write or speak in front of an audience.

There's a quote that I live by from Nathan Barry, "If you're feeling like an imposter, that means you're going in the right direction." When you doubt yourself or find yourself scared to go in a certain direction, you have to remind yourself you can't be afraid of trying something new. I feel that's your creative intuition nudging you in the direction of the artist you're supposed to become. Whether it's a successful or failed experiment, progress is progress and it'll lead you to the next step and chapter in your creative career.

Q: What do you think when people say, "It's who you know."?

A: I agree to an extent. I also believe you can create and attract your own opportunities but it does all stem from getting uncomfortable and showing up even when it's not convenient. I got out of my shell and made things happen. It's up to you to put yourself out there, kick out great work, and build those relationships that will hopefully lead to a job you love.

Fraser Davidson

Creative Director & Animator
Cub Studio

Fraser co-owns Cub Studio, an animation studio in London. He has nearly a decade of experience in the animation industry, having worked at Mainframe for six years prior to setting up the Sweet Crude collective. Fraser has won numerous awards for his animations and has worked with some of the world's biggest brands. His work with comedians on various projects has gained a great deal of acclaim and several million YouTube hits.

Q: What advice would you give a recent grad as they prepare their portfolio—especially animators?

A: I was fairly timid when it came to contacting companies, but the work I produced at school had an immediate commercial feel to it. The University projects I engaged with tended to be commercially oriented, and it allowed potential employers to see how I might fit into a working studio. You should make it short, to the point, and awesome. We understand that as a student your body of work is small. I'd rather watch 25–30s of an awesome reel than two minutes of padding.

Q: What is one of your pet peeves about designers fresh out of school?

A: Don't send a three paragraph email telling me about yourself. I don't mean to seem cruel or unnecessarily harsh, but I don't read them.

I do however look for a link and will watch 20 to 30 seconds of your reel. Drop us two lines explaining who you are, what you are looking for, include a link to your reel or best project. If your work is promising, I'll be more inclined to learn about your love of the outdoors, romantic walks on the beach, and love of Mexican food.

In an interview situation, it's important to come across as a competent person. Animation attracts a lot of introverts and people whose interests lie in technical proficiencies. I don't expect everyone to be the classic 'good communicators' with a bubbly personality. I do, however, expect potential employees to be straight-talking and enthusiastic about their work.

Q: What is something you notice about a animator's portfolio on first glance?

A: Originality and timing are the two things I look for. You can learn the technology, you can't learn to be original, to be humorous, or in my experience well-timed.

Q: What are the top three pieces you include in your portfolio?

A: The Guide to American Football, Trump Facts, FordPass showcase our company well. The Guide to American Football because we wrote, directed, and produced it. Trump Facts as its designed for social media, is short form, has a quick turnaround, and was responsive to current events. Finally, Ford is an interesting commercial piece for a great company that portrays our unique style.

www.cubstudio.com FrazDav cubstudio cubstudio cubstudio

Top and top left: *Self-initiated project, The Guide to American Football is a love letter to a sport Fraser wanted to share with a new audience.* **Middle:** *The Doc Brown piece is from a silly, comedic point of view.* **Bottom:** *Two screenshots from Trump Facts, designed for social media, is short form, has a quick turnaround, and was in response to current events.*

Peter Deltondo

Senior Experience Designer
GoFundMe

Since graduating, Peter has dabbled in many areas of design from branding to web design, but has landed and flourished in the User Experience arena. He is organized and enjoys motivating the designers on his team. Peter has run his own business as well as worked on teams as a Creative Director. From these experiences his communication skills and team-building skills have been honed and polished. He is comfortable presenting work to anyone, he knows how to interpret a client's desire and implement it to make everyone happy, and perhaps most importantly, he knows how to build and grow a team/company culture. Peter's position as the Creative Director at Mossio allowed him to sharpen his skills designing products with teams which set him up for his current position at GoFundMe. Product design is very different from web design, or other specialties of design.

Q: What are some strategies for showing an entire website or app in your portfolio?

A: I usually focus on one to three key screens for a project that's interesting and might attract a client's attention. Things with beautiful imagery, bold colors, and so forth. I haven't had a physical portfolio since I graduated from art school, and in my opinion no one should be using a physical portfolio anymore unless your type of work you want to do requires it.

Q: What is something you notice about a designer's portfolio at first glance?

A: If they are focused in one area of design or if they are more of a 'jack-of-all-trades' designer. I like hiring specialists. Personally, I focus on UI/UX websites, apps, and products. I have no interest in trying to do lettering, illustration, etc. Can I do it? Of course, but someone else can do it way better than me. Rather than be mediocre at those things, I'll hire or contract someone who does amazing work in whatever area I need to complete a project. If you're applying for a web design job, I don't care about what logos or flyers you created—that's not something I'll be looking for you to do. Make sure you're showing the type of work you want to be hired to do, or you'll never get hired to do it.

Q: How do you stage your portfolio pieces? With mock-ups that you purchase? Do you photograph your work yourself?

A: All of the above. I used to create mock-ups more frequently along with my photographer pal Alicja Colon and sell them on Creative Market. I still make custom mock-ups when required, but I also lean on the ease and convenience of purchasing a mock-up if it fits my purpose. I have a giant file called 'Potential Dribbble Shots' where I put the best files from my projects and then play around with various presentation styles. I probably spend 30–90 minutes per Dribbble shot testing out various presentation styles until I make a final decision. I'll show variations to friends to get feedback and if possible, try to animate the shot to show a little more of its interactive capabilities.

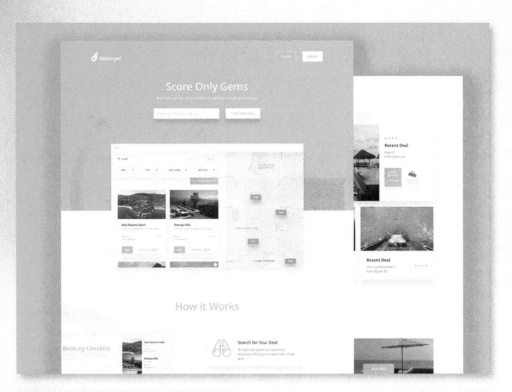

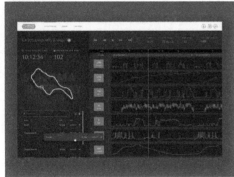

Top: *The BidAngel home page where Peter collaborated with Damian Kidd on the rebranding of this product.* **Bottom left:** *An app that measured car performance for the 2017 Prius Challenge. This was an early concept for the Race Strategy Editor. This tool allowed drivers prior to the race, to strategize how they would drive each section of the track on race day for maximum MPG.* **Bottom right:** *The Mossio team worked to created a small social network for the competing teams at the 2017 Prius Challenge.*

Shauna Lynn Panczyszyn

Hand Lettering Artist, Illustrator, Master Doodler

Full-time Freelancer

After graduating from the University of North Florida, Shauna worked as an intern at Brunet-García in Jacksonville, Florida, where she was able to work on numerous hand lettering projects. After the internship, a poster she had hand lettered at Brunet-García (The World of Foote) was accepted and published in Communication Arts Typography Annual 2 which has continued to bring her freelance jobs. In 2013, Shauna began freelancing full-time and she was regularly hired for her lettering style. She was one of four authors & artists for the book *Creative Lettering and Beyond* published in 2014. Her lettering and illustration style has been employed in packaging, branding, and advertising all over the world. By focusing on her lettering skills, practicing daily, and continually growing in a short period of time she has been able to land large national and international clients. Shauna was represented by agents as she first started in the field. In 2017 she left that business model and now personally handles all aspects of the business.

Q: **How has social media and networking played a role in making connections and landing jobs?**

A: It's played a huge part, I've connected with many people I may have not otherwise met. I am very active on Twitter and Instagram and a good number of my friendships in the industry started with me simply replying to a tweet or commenting on a project. I have received lettering work through friends being too busy to take on a job and passing it to me. I've also passed work to friends that I don't have time for or wasn't a good fit for. My rule is, if I wouldn't trust you to design for me, I can't refer you. I am selective of who I refer because it's a reflection on me.

Q: **What are things you did to help you grow your online audience and exposure?**

A: I post almost daily on Instagram, but I work to curate my feed so there's some cohesiveness to it. I will slip in a personal post to show I am still human, but I have seen more engagement on posts of my work because people follow me to see my lettering. I am active on Twitter, and that growth has been more from interacting with people on a regular basis and following people whose work and tweets I enjoy.

I keep my website updated with new work on a regular basis, updating it once a month depending on the quantity of work. I curate what goes on there because sometimes you get a project and it ends up just not looking how you hoped it would because the client made edits to it, so if I don't like the outcome of the work, I don't share it.

Top: *Personal Twitter Banner: Shauna regularly changes her social media to fit the seasons and uses it to experiment with new styles.* **Bottom left:** *For Light Grey Art Lab's SWARM group gallery show, Shauna illustrated the quote because she loves playing in the space between creepy and cute, and felt this would be a fun exploration into creepy children's book style art.* **Bottom right:** *Artists for Education is an organization aimed at bringing fun, engaging, and educational art to classrooms.*

www.shaunalynn.com shaunaparmesan shaunaparmesan shaunalynnpanczyszyn

Doc Reed

In-house Graphic Design Specialist

Premier Inc.

Doc graduated from East Carolina University with a BFA in Communication Art. He is a designer and illustrator with over 15 years experience in the field. Doc focuses on illustration, logo design, and branding. He has worked alongside big business and boutiques.

Q: Do you prefer an interviewee to present a digital portfolio or physical one?

A: Hands down digital. Especially if you're a web, animation, or motion designer. If you're a packaging designer, I'd like to see first-hand your skill level by looking at a physical product. If it's the first interview, send the digital to get a meeting. Once the door is opened, start a dialog, mention you have real pieces if they'd like to have a look. Have stellar photos in your book. I recommend a horizontal layout. People are typically going to be viewing these on laptops or desktops, so make them 1920x1080 or a 16:9 ratio.

Q: Do you have different curated portfolios for each type of client/employer?

A: You need to curate your portfolios! It's important you know why you're sending these particular examples to this company. Dig deeper for answers other than "I need a job." I've had great conversations with mentors and art directors about pulling pieces and focusing my portfolio. To know what pieces to include in your book, you need to know the job you want. Building your portfolio for the career you want is important. You need your portfolio to communicate clearly to art directors, "This is who I am. This is what I do. This is how I see myself working with your clients."

Q: What three things would you point to that will help students land a job?

A: Do 'passionate' projects and freelance. Try and gain experience doing the work you want to do. Work begets work. Build and foster honest relationships, keep an open mind, and always try to be a learner.

Q: What advice would you tell someone trying to break into the design and illustration?

A: Know what you want to do and fight to get there. Spend some time digging into who you are and who you want to be as a designer. When you go with the flow, you tend to end up somewhere way downstream. Write about what you're doing and share publicly so others can find you. Take the time to make goals.

Q: What is one of your pet peeves about designers that are fresh out of school?

A: Not being able to talk about your work is dangerous. As designers, we have to know why we made the decisions we made in our work. We are solving a problem. Not being able to explain those thoughts will be a hindrance in your career.

www.iamReedicus.com iamReedicus iamReedicus iamReedicus

Top: Light Cannon Films is a young, innovative company based in Wilmington, North Carolina. The goal was to portray Light Cannon Films as a warm, easy-going company without sacrificing professionalism. **Middle left:** This art print is inspired by one of Doc's favorite bands, The Avett Brothers. The goal here was to illustrate elements specific to the band, everything from the necklace worn to the patterns on the banjo. **Middle right:** This is a commemorative poster for the Hopscotch Music Festival. The concept was to show a familiar shape, the guitar, in a new and unfamiliar way. **Bottom right:** The Road to Damascus illustration based on a Bible passage for The Old & New Project.

T.J. Harley

President & Creative Director

Harley Creative

T.J. Harley got his start working in a t-shirt shop while attending Clemson University. He worked whenever he didn't have class and got a chance to learn to use Illustrator really well. After graduating he began working for The Collegiate Licensing Company in Atlanta, now IMG College. He worked at IMG as creative director for almost eleven years. T.J. now runs Harley Creative (HC), which focuses on the sports and entertainment industries.

Q: What piece of advice you would give a student as they prepare their portfolio?

A: One thing I would do is show as much variety of work as you can. You never know what a potential employer might respond to or need. If you try and put all of your eggs in one basket, be it all logo design, print, web, whatever, you may only attract employers who are looking for that specific skill set. If you can diversify your portfolio, you leave yourself open to more opportunities.

Q: What would you tell someone trying to break into the sports design industry?

A: Don't be an asshole. This business is all about relationships. There's plenty of talented people that can do the job as good, or better than you. Relationships are more important than talent. Be humble. If you're difficult to work with, clients will find someone else. It's that simple.

Put your head down, put the time in, practice, and work on getting better everyday.

Q: How do you prefer someone to apply for a job at your company?

A: For me a candidate would have to be someone that is good at a lot of different things. It might be a branding project one day, a web site another. I'd want someone who is flexible, can do everything well—and fast! A lot of the work I'm doing is on pretty stringent deadlines so the ability to work quickly and efficiently is something I look for. I also put a tremendous amount of stock in a respected colleague's recommendation. Almost 90% of my business comes from recommendations. If you are lucky enough to find a cheerleader, someone who really respects your work and wants to promote you there's no better advertising in the world.

Q: What three traits stand out to you as being particularly necessary or important?

A: Honesty. I try and be honest with my clients. At the end of the day I'm providing a service and I think it's important to tell clients what I think, even if that opinion isn't what they necessarily want to hear. **Listening.** It's always important to listen to people and be interested in what they're saying. It's not necessary to always be the one talking or controlling the conversation. **Flexibility.** A big reason why HC has been able to flourish is our ability to provide clients with different aspects of design, be it web, print, branding, social media, and so forth.

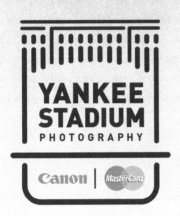

NACDA™

www.harley-creative.com 🐦 harley_creative 📷 harleycreative

Jennifer and Amy Hood

Cofounders and Creative Directors

Hoodzpah

Jen (left) and Amy (right) describe themselves as 'mutant humans' (twins) who have lived on both coasts and now call Newport Beach home. Wedged between the beach and the bay, they run their own design agency called Hoodzpah, specializing in branding. In 2011, they started their own agency because they felt they didn't look good on paper when trying to get hired. Having learned design via apprenticeship, they didn't have a formal four-year degree. Jen said, "we were also really young. No one was interested in hiring us. So we hired ourselves."

Q: When you are hiring a new designer what do you look for?

A: Good Attitude. Talent can be cultivated, but the right attitude is harder to teach. A positive, help-ful, interested attitude is harder to instill if not a predisposition. I look for someone who takes critique on their work easily, is not defensive, shows a genuine interest in what we do, and shows willingness to be of help in any way. **Being Proactive.** You'd be amazed how many people don't even know what we are working on or who our clients are when they interview. Re-search who you want to work for. Don't just try one email and give up. Even if someone says they aren't hiring, stay on their radar to show your interest is genuine, and that you continue to be interested for the long haul. Engage with the company and its employees on social, write

follow-up email to comment on good work they put out. Be in the forefront. Companies are busy and need gentle, positive reminders. When you get the job, don't always wait to be instructed on what to do. If you notice a problem or something causing your boss pain, solve that. Help out with that. This will get you promoted. Look for ways to make the business better and your boss' life easier. **Confidence.** Own your work. Don't be an egomaniac. But don't apologize for things when you're showing your portfolio. It's not a time for excuses. Show that you enjoy what you do. Show energy. Show passion. Don't blame a weakness in your work on your teacher or the prompt. **Design Intelligence.** Always. Answer. Why. Why did you make that design? Why did it solve the problem posed? Why was it the right solution for the audience? This data is what proves a design is good beyond subjective critique on the 'art' of it.

Q: Do you have a team helping you create the work?

A: We have a fluid team of freelancers on our agency roster, which we have vetted and use as skills fit projects. It keeps our company cul-ture true to principals we prize: everyone work-ing for us has the freedom to choose what to work on, to pick where they'll work from (and when—viva la midnight oil), and to say no to what doesn't suit their tastes or talents.

www.hoodzpahdesign.com thegoodhood inthegoodhood jenhood

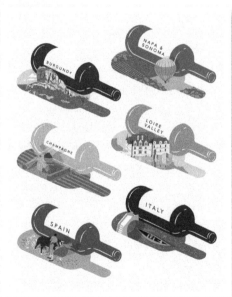

Top left: *The Stora Influencer branding system is a new Swedish Awards Show/Gala for Social Media Influencers. The main word their client used to describe what she wanted for the logo was 'Boss' and Luxe. The gold is gold foil and the turquoise and mint colors add a slightly modern touch.* **Top right:** *Logo system for Butterscotch including logo, monogram/ icon, and some secondary marks for use on coffee cups and signage.* **Middle right:** *Hoodzpah wanted to create a commemorative poster on 'Big Wednesday.' Big Wednesday is a day where waves were the biggest they have been in two decades! The waves and crowds were insane.* **Bottom left:** *illustration collaboration with both Jen and Amy for the* **Saute Magazine***. For a wine feature highlighting wines from various regions.*

Jason Craig

Senior Designer

Westobou & Freelancer

Jason relocated from the Midwest after dropping out of college to move to Augusta, Georgia. He has worked in the field of Graphic Design and Illustration since 1997 and has maintained a fine art career at the same time. Jason considers himself "a hands-on designer who has the responsibility to make other designers around him better through honest critique and peer mentorship." He splits his time between a full-time job, independent client work, and passion projects. Jason works for a music, art, and culture festival called Westobou where he is the Senior Designer creating print pieces, marketing, and maintaining the website. As an independent designer Jason works for a wide variety of clients. His favorite kind of project is spot illustration, but does a lot of branding and identities for bars, restaurants, beer companies, and nonprofits. In his free time he participates in an Art Collective called Pink Slips Analog, where he screen prints posters, creates hand-painted murals, and produces most of the merchandise that he sells.

Q: What advice would you give a recent grad as they prepare their portfolio?

A: Make it authentic. Only put work in your portfolio you want to get paid to do. I used to keep my illustration work out of my portfolio because I felt like it wasn't what I was being hired for. As a result, my portfolio looked very average and I never got hired as an illustrator which is what I really wanted to be. Make sure you include work that you are passionate about and not what you think will get you a job. Employers and team members want to see your passion.

Q: Do you prefer an interviewee to present a digital portfolio or physical one?

A: I am old school. I want to see the entire presentation. I want to see the details. How it is bound, how they hand it to me. How they act while I look at their work. These are the things that a client notices beyond the work you are hired to do. I have to assume you will make the same presentation to a client that you make to me. Everything is an opportunity.

Q: What would you tell someone never to do their first year on the job?

A: Never say 'can't.' Your first year at a job is when you will learn the most about the job and yourself. My dad says, "You are going to change this company when you come to work here and it is going to change you. If we are both happy with the result, you can stay." If there is anything that needs to be done—do it! Become the best at it. In the corporate world they call it 'ownership.' Do as much as possible in that first year and you will have a lot to talk about at your first annual review.

Q: What are some traits that have led to your success?

A: I've never met a stranger and I can talk to anyone and everyone. Be self-confident! Just because you've never done something before doesn't mean you can't do it. Be humorous. It's more fun to work with other fun people.

🐦 JasonKaleCraig   📷 jasonthe29th   🌐 jasonthe29th   f jasonthe29th

NASH FM / COUNTRY RADIO STATIONS

BECKS / OYSTER BAR

SBGC / NON PROFIT

INDIAN QUEEN / BAR

EMAIL INDUSTRIES / TECH FIRM

600 BROAD / ART GALLERY AND COMMUNITY CENTER

Top left: Six logos created for a variety of different businesses and nonprofits. **Top right:** Jason is a master at illustrating and communicating with a limited color palette. This event poster for the band, The Flaming Lips. **Middle:** Two color event poster for the band Lucero, illustrated, designed, and hand-printed. **Bottom left:** Two posters illustrated and designed for a Roller Derby series.

David O'Hara

Senior Product Designer

Axon

David earned a double major in Graphic Design and Commercial Art. After graduation David worked for an agency in Florida for three years then moved to Seattle, Washington where there was a larger design community and more opportunity for learning. While working for a new agency in Seattle, David became interested in User Experience design. He worked for Microsoft on the Office Labs team on their Microsoft Sway product as a UI/Visual Designer. He received an offer to go to Moz and work on two of their new products as a UX Designer and spent about two-and-a-half years there before coming to Axon. Axon works on an evidence and records management system for police agencies as well as body cam and Taser hardware.

Q: What qualities or skills are often overlook but have contributed significantly to your success?

A: Soft skills are one of the biggest factors for landing a job. It also is often the defining factor between a junior and senior level designer. Soft skills are your ability to connect with people and build lasting relationships that cultivate an atmosphere ideal for collaboration, creativity, and productivity.

Q: What advice would you give someone trying to break into the UX/UI field?

A: Read. Ask. Do. There are so many great articles and podcasts out there to learn about UX.

Medium.com is a treasure trove of great articles. If you live in a city with UX meetups, go! (Find these on meetups.com) It is a great opportunity to connect with other professionals, learn, and grow. After you read something, try it out. Tackle some small made up projects based on what you've learned. Find people who would be real-life users and test your ideas with them. The design community is made up of amazing people. Don't be afraid to ask many questions and ask for help. Those who have gone before you have been where you are and will give you great insight.

Q: How do you present your UX/UI work in your portfolio? Do you show multiple screens?

A: Show your process and tell a story. This is more important than the end result. This was a big thing I learned when transitioning from graphic design to UX Design. Everyone was just looking at the finished piece in your portfolio for graphic design. In UX, they more interested in the journey of how you arrived there, what you learned along the way, and what were the key decisions that changed the outcome. Share what you based your decisions on. Part of being a data-driven designer is learning how to track down data, understand what it is telling you, and make decisions based on that information. Make work that looks cohesive and well thought through. It's nice to have something to pass around in an interview, whether that is a prop to a story, a leave behind for each person in the room, or something that really drives home part of your presentation.

www.davidpohara.com   www.50statesapparel.com   davidpohara   davidpohara   davidpohara

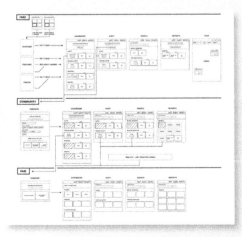

Top: *An initial phase of sketching for the Moz Content product.* **Middle left:** *Moz Content is a product built for content marketers to help them audit their content and track its performance as well as doing content discovery to inform their strategy. David worked on the product from its inception and was able to iterate on its features based on user data and research he gathered along the way.* **Middle right:** *Oly is a personal content assistant that helps collect and curate content. This is a detail of the concepting behind the logo.* **Bottom left:** *Working on the product architecture for Moz and designing the flow from the marketing funnel to establishing a tiered plan to encourage users to naturally convert to a paid user was a rewarding aspect of the project.*

Bob Ewing

Designer & Illustrator

Element Three

Bob Ewing is a designer and illustrator for Element Three (E3) in Indianapolis, Indiana. He is also a freelance lettering artist and co-owner of Inch x Inch, a nonprofit button club that supports youth art education.

Q: What did you do to land this job?

A: My friendship with Drew Hill got me in the door. He was already interviewing there and E3 was looking for someone else. Most design communities are small, never underestimate making real connections with people and where that can take you. You never know if where a friend or acquaintance works will be looking for a designer with your particular talents.

Secondly, the daily lettering project I started in September of 2013 gave me the confidence to take on some jobs I wouldn't have or couldn't have originally. I would have never had a portfolio good enough to get my current job.

Lastly, just be kind and work hard. The way you treat others and your work ethic will go a long way.

Q: How has social media played a role in establishing connections and landing new projects?

A: Social media has played a huge role in making connections and getting work. I would say most of my freelance work that isn't word of mouth comes through Instagram or Dribbble. I can't overstate the value of networking or building a community, I owe a lot to my community. Be human and make connections with real people. The online community is amazing and I have a lot of really great friends because of it, but make sure you connect with people in real life. You have to invest in people and it takes effort, you have to make that conscious decision.

Q: Can you explain how a designer's feed reflects their personality and values?

A: Companies do as much research as possible before hiring someone, including checking out your social media accounts. Whether it is your intention or not, social media is a snapshot of who you are.

Q: Let's say you recently started following a rising designer or illustrator, what might cause you to unfollow them?

A: Nudity, vulgar language, copying someone else's work, or simple immaturity.

Q: What was the best thing you did or have done that has helped you with building your confidence?

A: Make lots of work. Quantity leads to quality. Early on I had zero confidence in what I was making, it took quite a few years before I started to become confident in what I was creating. And still to this day I struggle with imposter syndrome and thinking what I am creating isn't good. Some days are better than others and that's okay.

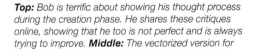

Top: Bob is terrific about showing his thought process during the creation phase. He shares these critiques online, showing that he too is not perfect and is always trying to improve. **Middle:** The vectorized version for the client and the final poster with Bob's illustration. **Bottom:** Element Three tasked Bob with creating the promos to advertise an event with Aaron Draplin.

www.bob-ewing.com   bobewing_   bobewing_   bobewing

Scott Biersack

Independent Lettering Artist, Illustrator, Graphic Designer, and Type Designer
Full-time Freelance

Scott's been freelancing for four years and doing it full-time for two years. His junior year of High School, Scott took a graphic design class and that class and especially his teacher helped him realize he wanted to pursue design as a career. He continued his education at Arizona State University where he received a Bachelors in Visual Communication Design. It was there his love for typography and type design was ignited. After graduation, Scott continued learning Type Design at the Cooper Union in New York City. He finished the year-long program in the summer of 2016; he moved back to Phoenix and has been freelancing ever since.

Q: What advice would you give a recent grad as they prepare their portfolio?

A: I know it has been said many times over but I highly agree to only include your best projects. Don't worry about numbers, it's all about quality over quantity. Additionally, only include projects of things you want to do more of. After graduation, students are left with a variety of projects—maybe an infographic, a website design, a branding project, etc. If you absolutely dread doing infographic design, don't include it in your portfolio. On the other hand, if you love branding work, include that and lots of it. It's beneficial to specialize in one particular thing than to be a jack-of-all-trades. In the working world, you're most likely going to have one role, not multiple (all depends on the job though).

Q: How has social media played a role in making connections and landing jobs?

A: Social media is the reason I am able to free-lance full-time! What would I do without it. It has brought about so many insanely cool opportunities. I share everything I create on social platforms, this allows art directors and creative directors to discover my work. I've been lucky enough to have never needed to go searching for the work. Thanks to social media, the work finds me.

Q: What advice would you tell someone trying to break into typography design and lettering?

A: The most important piece of advice I can give is the three P's: Practice, Persistence, and Patience. Whatever the skill, it doesn't necessarily need to even be design related, it will take time. Nothing comes overnight but with constant quality practice anyone can become good (and even great) at something.

The second piece of advice I can give is to ask yourself if you truly want to enter the lettering and typefield. Currently there are a lot of people doing it because it's 'trendy' and gets you 'follows' on social media. Those people and their work honestly don't progress as much as a person who loves what they're doing.

Top left: Gatefold Typeface Specimen Poster. **Top right:** The NYC piece was designed specifically for a Tuts Plus brush-script tutorial. **Middle right:** This invitation was designed specifically to invite guests to attend the annual Art Directors Club Paper Expo. The piece was inspired by vintage book covers of the 19th century. **Bottom right:** Custom lettering piece for Scott's new type foundry, Continental Type Co. **Bottom:** Scott was invited to participate in Type Hike Poster, a tribute to the National Parks Service centennial. He selected Hawaii's Volcanoes National Park.

Resources

Ad Week | adweek.com
An advertising trade publication that covers creativity, client–agency relationships, global advertising, accounts in review, and new campaigns.

Adobe Color CC | color.adobe.com
The color wheel in Adobe Color CC is designed to help you with color palette selection in an intuitive manner by using presets that are based on color theory rules.

AIGA | aiga.org
The professional organization for design. AIGA is the profession's oldest and largest professional membership organization for design.

Behance | behance.net
The leading online platform to showcase and discover creative work. The creative world updates their work in one place to broadcast it widely and efficiently.

Bittbox | bittbox.com
A website where you can obtain high-quality design assets, tutorials, articles, Photoshop brushes, and textures.

CMYK Magazine | cmykmag.com
A magazine featuring quarterly contests for emerging artists and designers who focus on art direction, copywriting, design, photography, and illustration.

COLOURLovers | colourlovers.com
COLOURlovers is a creative community where people from around the world create and share colors, palettes, and patterns, discuss the latest trends, and explore colorful articles.

Communication Arts Magazine | commarts.com
A magazine that includes design, advertising, illustration, photography, and interactive annuals, as well as design trends, color predictions, articles, and book reviews.

Creative Market | creativemarket.com
Creative Market is an online marketplace for community-generated design assets. The company sells graphics, WordPress themes, stock photography, and other digital goods for use by web creatives.

Design Matters | debbiemillman.com/designmatters
Design Matters is a podcast founded and hosted by American writer, educator, artist, and designer Debbie Millman.

Design Observer | designobserver.com
A website that features news and critical essays on design, urbanism, social innovation, and popular culture.

Design Recharge | rechargingyou.com
Design Recharge is a weekly web show devoted to inspiring, connecting, and educating designers.

Design Seeds | design-seeds.com
Design Seeds has evolved into an international community who share a passion for creating color palettes inspired by images submitted through Instagram.

The Dieline | thedieline.com
The Dieline highlights the importance and value of packaging design for brands in today's world. They provide a platform where the community can examine projects, learn more about the design process, and stay informed of trends.

Dribbble | dribbble.com
Dribbble is a community where web designers, graphic designers, illustrators, icon artists, typographers, logo designers, and other creative types share small screenshots (shots) that show their work, process, and current projects.

Font Squirrel | fontsquirrel.com
Font Squirrel is a great resource for free, hand-picked, high-quality, commercial-use fonts.

GD USA Magazine | gdusa.com
A magazine that provides information on graphic design news, trends, people, ideas, contests, and products from the design community.

GraphicRiver | graphicriver.net
GraphicRiver is part of Envato Market. On GraphicRiver you can buy and sell royalty-free, layered Photoshop files, vectors, icon packs, Adobe add-ons, and design templates.

How Magazine | howdesign.com
A magazine that helps designers to be more creative and connected. Their mission is to serve the business, creativity, and technology needs of graphic designers.

Klo Portfolios | kloportfolios.com
Klo Portfolios makes high-quality custom screwpost portfolio books for creatives and professionals.

Kristin Dunn | kdbooks.com
Kristin Dunn bookbinding and design offers a large selection of ready-to-ship, customizable presentation products. From clamshell boxes to screw post portfolios you are sure to find a unique and personalized solution.

Lynda.com | lynda.com
Lynda.com is a leading online learning platform that helps anyone learn business, software, technology, and creative skills to achieve personal and professional goals.

The Noun Project | thenounproject.com
The Noun Project is a website that aggregates and catalogs symbols that are created and uploaded by graphic designers around the world.

Pina Zangaro | pinazangaro.com
As a leading-edge manufacturer of presentation materials, Pina Zangaro has been marking trends and producing a line of products to support the next generation of artwork.

Pixeden | pixeden.com
Pixeden is a one-stop place for all the tools that a designer might need in his or her day-to-day routine. Pixeden thrives to bring you the best of the best for paid and free graphic, web, and design resources.

Pixelbuddha | pixelbuddha.net
Pixelbuddha is passionate about creating free and premium resources for the professional design community.

Print Magazine | printmag.com
Print is a bimonthly magazine about design that places contemporary visual culture in its social, political, and historical context.

PSDCovers | psdcovers.com
Download high-resolution Photoshop actions for product mock-ups for your web and graphic projects.

Skillshare | skillshare.com
Skillshare is an online learning community where anyone can discover, take, or even teach a class.

Slack | slack.com
A platform that connects teams with the apps, services, and resources they need to get work done. Find slack channels in your niche area, find them in your city, and connect with like-minded people.

Smashing Magazine | smashingmagazine.com
Smashing Magazine is a website and publisher that offers editorial content and professional resources for web developers and web designers.

Stack Skills | stackskills.com
StackSkills is an online learning center built where you can enroll in courses on topics from coding, to design, to business.

Squarespace | squarespace.com
Squarespace is a software as a service-based content management system website builder, blogging platform, hosting service, commerce platform, and domain name registrar.

Subtle Patterns | toptal.com/designers/subtlepatterns
Subtle Patterns (a collection of seamless background patterns) have been used by many blogs and websites world wide, even big corporations have used Subtle Patterns.

Treehouse | teamtreehouse.com
Treehouse brings affordable technology education to people everywhere in order to help them achieve their dreams and change the world.

Tuts+ | tutsplus.com
As part of Envato's creative ecosystem, Envato Tuts+ contributes to our mission of "helping people learn and earn online."

TypeEd | type-ed.com
TypeEd's is a program designed to educate designers about the fundamental theory of type, build a typographic foundation of practice, so they can preserve the integrity of visual communication.

Typespiration | typespiration.com
Free inspirational web font combinations with color palettes and ready-to-use HTML and CSS code.

Typewolf | typewolf.com
Typewolf is an independent typography resource created by Jeremiah Shoaf.

Udemy | udemy.com
Udemy is a global marketplace for learning and teaching online where students are mastering new skills and achieving their goals by learning from an extensive library of over 55,000 courses taught by expert instructors.

Unsplash | unsplash.com
Unsplash is a website dedicated to sharing copyright-free photography under the Unsplash license.

Weebly | weebly.com

Weebly is a web-hosting service featuring a drag-and-drop website builder.

Wix | wix.com

Wix is a cloud-based web development platform that allows users to create HTML5 web sites and mobile sites through the use of online drag and drop tools.

WordPress | wordpress.com

WordPress is an online, open source website creation tool. It's an easy-to-use, yet powerful blogging and content management system.

Credits

All photos reprinted by permission. Photo credits are assigned to the page in which the image first appears.

132 @twinsterphoto/shutterstock.com
@Shablon/shutterstock.com

138 @Rawpixel.com/shutterstock.com
Modified by Ben Hannam.

143 @Anatoly Maslennikov/
shutterstock.com

151 @garagestock/shutterstock.com

152 @leedsn/shutterstock.com

155 Copyright © 2017 by Colin Tierney.
Copyright © 2017 by Prapasara
Tubhirun.
@rvlsoft/shutterstock.com

159 Copyright © 2017 by Zachary Smith.

161 Copyright © 2017 by Hebah
Abdelqader.
@rvlsoft/shutterstock.com

162 Copyright © 2017 by Nick Brito.
Copyright © 2017 by Meagan
Apperson.

166 Copyright © 2017 by Karina Carter.

169 Copyright © 2017 by Rocky Roark.
@rvlsoft/shutterstock.com

170 Copyright © 2017 by Elaina Mastrilli.

174 @Matthew Jacques/shutterstock.com
Modified by Ben Hannam.

176 Copyright © 2017 by Bethany Heck.
@one AND only/shutterstock.com

177 Copyright © 2017 by Bethany Heck.

178 Copyright © 2017 by Matt Vergotis.
@Natalie Zakharova/shutterstock.com

179 Copyright © 2017 by Matt Vergotis.
@rvlsoft/shutterstock.com

180 Copyright © 2017 by Von Glitschka.
@29october/shutterstock.com

181 Copyright © 2017 by Von Glitschka.

182 Copyright © 2017 by Dustin Lee.

@OoddySmile Studio/shutterstock.com

183 Copyright © 2017 by Dustin Lee.

184 Copyright © 2017 by Nikki Villagomez.

185 Copyright © 2017 by Nikki Villagomez.

186 Copyright © 2017 by Johnny Gwin.
Copyright © 2017 by Holly Murphy.

187 Copyright © 2017 by Johnny Gwin.

188 Copyright © 2017 by Drew Hill.

189 Copyright © 2017 by Drew Hill.

190 Copyright © 2017 by Scotty Russell.

191 Copyright © 2017 by Scotty Russell.

192 Copyright © 2017 by Fraser Davidson.

193 Copyright © 2017 by Fraser Davidson.

194 Copyright © 2017 by Peter Deltondo.

195 Copyright © 2017 by Peter Deltondo.

196 Copyright © 2017 by Shauna Lynn
Panczyszyn.

197 Copyright © 2017 by Shauna Lynn
Panczyszyn.

198 Copyright © 2017 by Doc Reed.
Copyright © 2017 by Tyler LaCross.

199 Copyright © 2017 by Doc Reed.

200 Copyright © 2017 by T.J. Harley.

201 Copyright © 2017 by T.J. Harley.

202 Photos courtesy of Zuzanna
Gerulewicz. Copyright © 2017 by
Jennifer Hood and Amy Hood.

203 Copyright © 2017 by Jennifer Hood
and Amy Hood.

204 Copyright © 2017 by Jason Craig.
Copyright © 2017 by Justin Blair.

205 Copyright © 2017 by Jason Craig.

206 Copyright © 2017 by David O'Hara.
Copyright © 2017 by Josh Mortenson.

207 Copyright © 2017 by David O'Hara.

208 Copyright © 2017 by Bob Ewing.

CPSIA information can be obtained
at www.ICGtesting.com
Printed in the USA
LVHW06s2030230318
571016LV00007B/37/P

9 781524 943974